Introduction

Lean for Practitioners has been designed to be read by busy healthcare professionals first time in around half a day or less, but also to be a useful guide and reference for use throughout your journey to Lean.

The focus of the book is on providing the essential information required to kick-start your knowledge of Lean and how it applies in a healthcare setting. It does not go into the detailed theories that underpin many of the concepts as this would significantly increase the size of the book and defeat my primary objective of making the contents accessible to the widest group of people working in healthcare organisations.

The idea for this short book came originally from the various lectures and seminars where I was asked to provide practical information on how to use Lean in healthcare organisations. These presentations evolved into a series of checklists and guides that were given away as part of the support provided by me to our client organisations.

Over time, as these original guides and checklists were passed on, more and more people began to ask for them until it became obvious that there was a need for a simple introduction to using Lean in healthcare, and that is when *Lean for Practitioners* was born.

The book itself evolves all the time as I find new and better ways of explaining Lean in healthcare and as new projects and examples of best practice are completed. On behalf of the clients I have supported, my team and colleagues and those who have taken the time to review this book, I would like to welcome you to the sixth edition of *Lean for Practitioners*.

Contents

Chapter 1

So, what is this thing called Lean?

At its heart, Lean is simply a philosophy designed to help organisations systematically identify and eliminate activities and processes that are preventing them from being effective. I tend to refer to Lean as 'structured common sense' as it is something that anyone can understand and apply to their work areas and processes.

Lean can also provide a structure for continuous improvement, and this is where it can help to start changing the way that the organisation behaves and the way it responds to problems and opportunities.

As a concept, Lean is very easy to understand and that is both a blessing and a curse. Whilst it is good that people can quickly appreciate the benefits of Lean, applying the tools and concepts effectively to real-life situations can take a lot of practice. The fact that Lean is 'easy in the head, but harder in the hand' is at the root of many failed 'Lean' programmes where people give up too soon. In addition, many people who 'do Lean' only ever learn one or two tools (usually 5S and Process Analysis), and because of this limited exposure to Lean they put Lean in a mental category called something like 'tactical tool' and underestimate or fail to realise what can really be achieved by using it when you apply it to a whole organisation.

Although some people think of Lean as a modern management

fad it has a long history that we explore in more detail in Appendix 9. For most purposes, Lean can be shown to have evolved out of the improvement system used by Toyota and what was called the Toyota Production System (TPS). This was developed in the 1950s and the father of TPS (and one could therefore argue the grandfather of Lean) was Toyota's Chief Production Engineer, Taiichi Ohno. It was he who first systematically reviewed what the company was doing and found that much of it was not adding any value to the end customer and was instead tying up resources wastefully – and it was under his guidance that the tools and approaches evolved to enable the employees at Toyota to spot these 'non-value adding activities' and make improvements.

The Toyota Production System drove Toyota's strategy and the way the whole organisation behaved. One of the first ways that later adopters of Toyota's approach modified this approach was to focus it purely on short-term fixes, and therefore many missed out on the long-term organisational change it can drive.

In the mid-90s, James Womack and Dan Jones wrote the book *Lean Thinking* which provided details of how the Toyota Production System could be applied in manufacturing. In many ways Lean is the wrong word to have used as to most people it means 'cutting to the bone' or 'devoid of excess fat' as opposed to its correct interpretation of 'designed for the customer' and 'flexible and robust', but the name 'Lean' has stuck and is recognisable to many in healthcare organisations, and it therefore the term I will use throughout this book.

So is there a need for Lean in healthcare? Well, when you look at the processes and pathways experienced by patients and service users you find that many are fundamentally broken. This does not mean necessarily that the care being provided is poor, but the time taken to access a professional, and the costs associated with accessing advice and care, can be excessive and fraught with risks and errors which can range from the patient receiving incorrect dates for clinics through to incorrect procedures and tests being carried out.

In a manufacturing context as well as in a healthcare context the focus is on delivering what the customer wants with the minimum of waste (in terms of time, cost, resources, etc.), and that is what most people want to achieve anyway in healthcare. So why can it be so difficult to achieve this optimum solution and why are the processes so difficult to manage?

The reason why this happens is often because things have changed since the process was first introduced, such as new clinical practice, changes in mandatory reporting or the introduction of a new IT system, and the process now no longer functions in the way it was designed to. Another common reason for problems is that the process was designed in isolation (for example, designed by the outpatient team without reference to primary care colleagues) and therefore the process has created problems either upstream or downstream of the process that causes it to not work effectively.

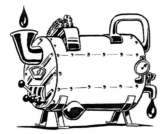 Using a mechanical example, when the processes were first designed they felt like an 'efficient machine' that ran smoothly and did not waste energy but then...

...the reality sets in. The first issues found are those that were 'built in' to the machine, such as forgetting to involve others. Later on, the effects of changes in best practice, new reporting requirements, statutory targets, etc., wear the machine down further until the energy required to run the machine becomes excessive and the machine breaks down a lot.

Many people in healthcare organisations say that they feel that they are working harder today than they used to and yet are still only getting the same or worse results, and this is often even true for those teams who have had increases in headcount.

Using Lean to design healthcare processes helps you avoid building in problems, mostly by focusing on the 'end-to-end' pathway or process rather than just one part of it, and also by helping you create a process of continuous improvement so that you are ready and can cope with the changes that are bound to happen, from a new target to a change of clinical practice and from new medical technology to a new phone system.

Lean states that all activities within a given organisation can be broken down into two basic types: those that are adding value to customers and those that are not. These latter 'Non-Value Adding activities' are also called Muda or Wastes and are at the bottom of many problems related to quality, productivity and capacity in healthcare organisations.

Value Adding (VA) activities are those activities that the customer 'wants' and would be prepared to pay for (if they had to). By contrast, Non-Value Adding (NVA) activities are those activities which tie up cost/time/resources but add no value to the customer (whoever they may be) and for which the customer would be reluctant to pay for (if they had to).

Therefore, at its simplest level, Lean is a philosophy that enables organisations to categorise (or 'see') Non-Value Adding activities and then eliminate them.

An important concept in Lean is that we have to start with the belief that it is always the process that is broken or faulty and not the people working within it. This statement may seem very simplistic, but if we start with the alternative assumption, that individuals are at fault, we will encounter resistance at every step, and in reality experience has shown that it really is normally the process that is broken anyway.

You may ask at this point, 'Surely not all the problems can arise from process issues? What about human error?' Well, Lean can also be used to design processes that minimise the risk of human error. Think about how different connectors reduce the risk of the wrong gases being fed to a patient, or how consistently using the same drug record throughout a patient's journey reduces the risk of medication error arising. This does not mean that Lean can create a perfectly safe service that is free from the risk of human error but it can create processes that are less likely to encounter problems and where people are less likely to make mistakes as well as creating processes to learn from every incident and ensure that controls and improvements are put in place to reduce the risk of further problems occurring.

In this chapter I have attempted to introduce you to the idea that Lean is neither new nor purely tactical. In the following chapters I will introduce the basics of Lean and show how they can easily be introduced in any healthcare organisation. In the next chapter we will explore the concepts and some of the terminology of Lean.

Chapter 1 Self Assessment Questions

• **Who was Taiichi Ohno?**

• **Name the two main types of activities that Lean helps you to identify**

• **Who gave Lean its name?**

• **What does TPS stand for?**

Chapter 2

The Key Lean Concepts

In this chapter we expand further on the concepts of Value Adding and Non-Value activities as introduced earlier and explore the basic principles and concepts that underpin Lean.

Value Adding (VA) & Non-Value Adding (NVA) Activities

As already mentioned, Lean breaks all activities down into only two types: those that are Value Adding (VA) and those that are Non-Value Adding (NVA) to the customer.

Value Adding (VA) activities are defined as those that the customer 'wants' to happen, is aware of and would be prepared to 'pay for' (if appropriate). Typical Value Adding activities for patients within healthcare organisations include:

- ⊙ Accurate information

- ⊙ Timely treatment

- ⊙ Effective treatment

- ⊙ Swift and safe discharge

- ⊙ Respect and dignity

- ⊙ Access to care

However, the only way to determine whether something is Value Adding or not is to and listen to what is called the VotC (Voice of the Customer).

Non-Value Adding (NVA) (also known as 'Waste' or 'Muda') activities are things that the customer does not want or does not care about and for which they would not be prepared to 'pay for' if they had to. We will explore the different categories of NVA later, but before we do we need to see the impact they have in a healthcare environment.

In a typical healthcare process, Non-Value Adding activities far outweigh the Value Adding ones with the latter often accounting for less than 10% of the steps in a typical pathway and an even smaller amount of the elapsed time. In the following example we will review an everyday process and look at those steps that are perceived as Value Adding by the patient. Obviously, if we look at the process from another viewpoint we will find that the steps that are seen as Value Adding will change, and being clear about who the customer is and exactly what they want is a key Lean concept.

- **Start – Patient feels unwell**

- NVA – Books appointment to see General Practitioner

- NVA – Waits for appointment

- NVA – Drives to appointment and waits for session

- **VA – GP session undertaken and treatment plan created including referral to secondary care**

- NVA – Patient drives home

- ● NVA – Patient waits for appointment to be made

- ● NVA – Referral received at secondary care organisation and processed

- ● **VA – Consultant grades and accepts referral**

- ● NVA – Letter returned to referral centre for letter to be produced and sent

- ● NVA – Patient receives letter

- ● NVA – Patient has to ring to confirm appointment

- ● NVA – Patient waits for date of outpatient appointment

- ● NVA – Patient drives to outpatient appointment

- ● NVA – Patient checks in and waits

- ● **VA – Patient taken in to see consultant and the need for diagnostic testing identified**

- ● NVA – Patient puts in request for diagnostic testing and checks out

- ● NVA – Patient goes home and waits...

Now, we could go on through the whole process and we will find the same pattern of a few Value Adding activities surrounded by extended periods of Non-Value Adding activity for the patient.

As already mentioned, we can look at this process in a completely different way by changing the 'customer' to nurses, doctors, pharmacists, administrators, etc. and whilst the steps that are seen as Value Adding may change, we would still find the same pattern of a few Value Adding activities surrounded by lots of Non-Value Add. It is not uncommon for healthcare professionals to spend less than 30% of every working day providing real care or service. Again, we must assume that it is the process that is broken and causes this level of performance, and again experience shows that generally this is a correct assumption.

Even though it is apparently simple to say that activities are either Value Adding or Non-Value Adding this differentiation causes a lot of problems in reality. Sometimes the confusion arises because people are not clear who the customer is, sometimes there is confusion because people do not want to believe that what they are doing might be Non-Value Adding, but more often than not the confusion arises because people think that things cannot be changed and therefore they must be Value Adding. Here are a couple of examples that have caused problems for people in the past:

- I have to collect the swabs from the store four times per shift. If I do not go to get them they will not arrive and therefore the task must be Value Adding.

- I have to copy the information on our computer screen onto the patient notes. If I did not do it they would not be in the notes and therefore the task must be Value Adding.

What we can say about the first example above is that in going to get the swabs you are just moving and the customer (whether that is a clinician or a patient) is not getting any value from you moving to and fro and therefore it is Non-Value Adding.

In the second example above, why would the customer be happy with you copying information from a computer into their records? What about having a printer or even having electronic records? Again, this is really a Non-Value Adding activity.

These examples show why it is important to state that just because something has to be done today does not make it automatically Value Adding.

This is an essential concept as without it every activity will be seen as Value Adding, and the reality of Lean is that you always attack the Non-Value Adding activity and rarely (if ever) look to tackle the Value Adding activities, because tackling Value Adding activities normally involves making people rush or lots of money.

There are categories of Non-Value Adding (such as checks or certain tests) that you may never eliminate or may not want to eliminate but which are fundamentally not Value Adding. These could be termed 'Essential Non-Value Adding' activities but if you were to create this 'third' category (the other two being Value Adding and Non-Value Adding) these activities will be treated exactly as Value Adding tasks, and therefore there will be little incentive to change or improve the way they are done.

In reality, if something is Non-Value Adding it should be stated as such because there is a second important point to mention in that when a task is considered Non-Value Adding it gives us the right to challenge the way it is done and does not mean it is automatically going to be removed.

As already mentioned, we do have some help in determining whether something is Aalue Adding or not by listening to the

VotC (Voice of the Customer). This requires us to speak to the customers (who in healthcare environments are predominantly, but not exclusively, patients) about what they view is Aalue Adding or not.

We can further test whether something is Value Adding by passing it through the following test:

1. Does the customer value the service/activity? (Do they want it to happen?)

2. Does the customer 'experience' the service/activity? (Are they aware of it?)

3. Is it **impossible** to remove or change the service/activity without the customer noticing

If the answer is 'Yes' to all three of the above, the activity can be classed as Value Adding. If the answer is no to any of them, then the item is likely to be Non-Value Adding.

It is a fact that you will spend a long time discussing which activities are Value Adding and which are Non-Value Adding and this should be viewed as a healthy and helpful debate, although it may not feel like it when you have those discussions.

The New & Old 7 Wastes

When he was developing the Toyota Production System, Taiichi Ohno spent time trying to categorise the types of Non-Value Adding activity that were present within the process. This was finally coded into the original (or old) '7 Wastes' (or Seven Deadly Sins) which were stated for a manufacturing company as:

- **Over-production** – producing more than is required

- **Waiting** – waiting for things to happen, finish or start

- **Inventory** – holding more stock than is required

- **Transport** – moving and handling materials and items

- **Motion** – the movement of equipment and people

- **Rework** – having to repeat tasks or correct errors

- **Over-processing** (or processing waste) – undertaking activities that are not required

Since then, it has become obvious that there is in fact an eighth waste, that being the waste of human talent.

Two of the original wastes (Motion & Transport) are closely related. Motion is the waste of human movement and Transport is the waste of moving 'things' (products, materials, etc.). By grouping Motion & Transport together, changing the words used to better suit a healthcare environment and adding in the eighth Waste (Talent) we can organise the original 7 Wastes into a new set of 7 Wastes that spell the word 'WORMPIT':

○ **W**aiting – waiting for things to start or arrive.

○ Over-Processing – this is doing more activity than is required.

○ Rework – also known as correction, this is about repeating activities because of a problem.

○ Motion (& Transport) – motion is the movement of humans and transport the movement of things.

○ Processing Waste – doing things that don't need to be done.

○ Inventory – stacking information, materials or patients.

○ Talent – misusing the skills of individuals or teams.

As already mentioned, these Non-Value Adding activities are also referred to as Muda or Wastes and we can review some examples of each in a healthcare context below:

○ **Waiting** – examples include time spent by patients waiting to be seen by a healthcare professional, or for healthcare professionals waiting for information or equipment to arrive.

○ **Over-Processing** – examples include repeatedly gathering information from patients or repeating blood tests.

○ **Rework** – (aka Correction) examples include chasing up missing information or having to deal with a secondary infection or other unexpected outcome.

- ○ **Motion (& Transport)** – examples include patients travelling back and forth to healthcare facilities or having to move consumables around a hospital.

- ○ **Processing Waste** – examples include undertaking unnecessary tests or completing detailed reports when a simple summary will do.

- ○ **Inventory** – examples include bringing all patients in at 9am even though some may not be seen till 3pm, or bringing 20 boxes of gloves up to a ward where they cannot be stored when only 5 boxes are used per week.

- ○ **Talent** – examples include nurses moving trolleys and receptionists being asked to screen and prioritise patients.

The 5 Lean Principles

In the book *Lean Thinking* by Dan Jones and Jim Womack the authors identified five 'Key Principles of Lean Systems and Organisations', and whilst we need to consider differences between manufacturing and healthcare when it comes to implementation, the five principles are still extremely useful in helping us create a framework for understanding Lean in healthcare.

The 5 Principles of Lean

| Value | Value Stream | Flow | Pull | Perfection |

The details of each of the principles are shown below.

1st Principle: Value – understand what your customer 'values'

The first principle is concerned with listening to the Voice of the Customer (VotC) and determining what the customer perceives as Value Adding. In a healthcare context, patients and service users are normally the primary customer, but there could be others who are important. One recommendation is to identify who your 'prime' customer groups are (no more than three) and then to work out what each customer group sees as Value Adding.

2nd Principle: Value Stream[1] – understand how you currently deliver value to your customer

Having identified what your customers view as Value Adding you must then understand how you deliver this value by analysing the steps in the 'Value Stream' that converts inputs to outputs such as helping patients who are unwell (inputs) to become well again (outputs). I will return to this issue of Value Streams later in this book

3rd Principle: Flow – eliminate bottlenecks and constraints so that the value can 'flow'

Having understood how you currently deliver value (i.e. the Value Stream), the next principle is to make the value 'flow' by eliminating bottlenecks, bringing Value Adding steps closer together (both in terms of physical distance and the time between steps), eliminating 'batching' and queuing of activities and moving towards a process where value 'flows' continuously.

---

1 'Pathway' is the commonly used healthcare term that means the same as Value Stream

I have shown a process below that I believe flows. It is based on a local 'hand car washing' facility near to where I live. The basic process takes 6 minutes and consists of three stages: Wash the Car, Wax/Shampoo and Rub In/Dry. Each step takes approximately 2 minutes and the equipment required for each step is located in the right place. Through this process the team can clean up to 30 cars per hour.

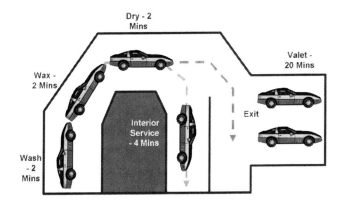

For the majority of cars (around 80–85% of cars), they will then drive straight out after the wash. A smaller number of cars (around 15%) will also require an interior service (vacuum and window clean) that lasts 4 minutes and they have designed the process so that the minority of cars who want an interior service do not stop the main 'flow' of customers who just want an exterior wash. Lastly, on a very few occasions (<5%) customers will want a valet service that lasts around 20 minutes, and whilst not part of the main process, the wash team have an area where they can 'park' these cars on the rare occasions that they arise.

However, the main process is built to manage the flow of the 'bulk' of the customers (those requiring only the 6-minute wash), which is an important Lean concept.

In Lean terminology, it is common to talk about Runners, Repeaters and Strangers. Runners are activities that occur all the time, the 'common' activities. Repeaters are less common but still occur regularly. Strangers are rare or 'odd ball' activities that only arise occasionally.

In the example given, the basic 6-minute wash is the 'Runner', the wash plus 4-minute interior clean is the 'Repeater' and the 20-minute valet is a 'Stranger', and the process is designed around the Runners and Repeaters as they form the bulk of the work to be done and therefore have the biggest impact on the ability of the process to 'flow'.

In a healthcare context the same principles apply, namely design the process around the most likely scenarios or conditions as this will give you the best return on your investment. This does not mean that you ignore the Strangers, but normally there are thousands upon thousands of activities or conditions that 'might' arise and to design a process that copes with them all would be impossible, whereas the most likely conditions arise every day of the week and therefore, in the long run, tie up substantially more resource/time/effort than an event that might occur only once a year or less frequently.

4th Principle: Pull – keep the process flowing by triggering activity only on demand

The fourth Lean principle is concerned with keeping the process flowing by triggering activity on demand and 'pulling' people and equipment through the process. The idea of 'Pull' in a healthcare context is to keep the process working by drawing resources/patients/materials to the point at which they are needed to prevent the process stopping and having to wait for it to arrive.

To illustrate this, I will use an example of a 'Pull' system that I saw operating in an Outpatients Clinic (specifically a Rheumatology Clinic). I have created a representation of the clinic in the figure below.

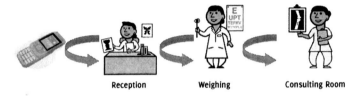

| Reception | Weighing | Consulting Room |

The aim of the 'Pull' was to keep the clinic 'flowing' and to maximize the consultant's utilisation. In this example, as one patient left the consulting room, a patient who had already been weighed and is ready to be seen is 'pulled' into see the consultant. This triggers another patient to be 'pulled' from the waiting area by a nurse so that the patient can be weighed and made ready to see the consultant as soon as the previous patient leaves the consulting room. Before all of this, 24 hours prior to the appointment, patients are 'pulled' via a text message to remind them to attend.

5th Principle: Perfection – drive for continuous improvement

The last principle is concerned with creating an environment that continuously strives for perfection. This will mean looking for further improvements in the process and dealing with issues and problems that arise. This is often the principle that is overlooked when people think they have 'gone Lean' but is the most important principle as it drives continuous improvement.

The Hierarchy of Improvement

The 'Hierarchy of Improvement' is a useful three stage process that is used in Lean projects to help teams to identify and prioritise improvements:

- Aim first to **Eliminate** the Non-Value Adding activity by getting rid of it completely

- If you can't eliminate it, can you **Reduce** the size (or impact) of the Non-Value Adding activity

- If you can't reduce it, can you **Combine** it with another activity

When approaching improvements, the focus should always be on eliminating Non-Value Adding activities as this will release the most resources (people, time, money, etc.) and often reduces risk by the greatest percentage.

If you cannot completely eliminate the activity, then the next step is to look at the possibility of reducing it – for example reducing the amount of information required to be completed or reducing the distance travelled.

Lastly, if you cannot reduce it, the third step is to explore whether you can combine the activity with another one so that it becomes less of a burden on the organisation, although the benefit of this is often less than reducing the task and much less than the elimination of the task completely.

It is sometimes possible to combine the second and third priorities – for example, first reducing an activity and then combining two activities together to get even more benefit!

Earlier in this chapter I mentioned the issue of 'Essential Non-Value Adding' activities. These are activities that are fundamentally Non-Value Adding but which you cannot or do not want to eliminate. The hierarchy of improvement (Eliminate, Reduce and Combine) allows you to look at Reducing or Combining these activities without having to Eliminate them – and it is for this reason that I suggested you should never be tempted to treat them as anything other than Non-Value Adding.

Chapter 2 Key Concepts Summary

Value Adding (VA)
Something they are aware of, something they want and something that is essential to the process.

Non-Value Adding (NVA)
Something that ties up resources/money/time and which is not something the customer wants and/or cares about.

Waste/Muda
Alternative names for things which are Non-Value Adding.

Essential Non-Value Adding
Activities that are fundamentally Non-Value Adding but which you may not be able to eliminate (or may not want to) but that are still candidates for being reduced or combined with other activities.

VotC (Voice of the Customer)
(Pronounced Voit-Ka) The process of understanding exactly what the customer of the process sees as Value Adding.

WORMPIT Wastes

The acronym for the key Non-Value Adding activities that can be found in healthcare organisations.

Eliminate, Reduce, Combine

A hierarchy of how you should approach addressing of Non-Value Adding activities in a Lean system – first try to eliminate the activity, if you can't eliminate it then reduce it and if you can't reduce it, can you combine it with another activity?

5 Principles of Lean

These define the five principles of a Lean process, which are: Value, Value Stream, Flow, Pull and Perfection.

Chapter 2 Self Assessment Questions

• What are the 5 Principles of Lean?

• Identify an example from your organisation for each of the
  WORMPIT Non-Value Adding categories

• What does VotC stand for?

• What is missing from this sequence:
  Eliminate, _____ , Combine?

Chapter 3

Step by Step Guide to 'Going Lean'

This chapter provides a step by step approach to introducing
Lean and is designed to provide readers with a basic framework
to work with. The five-step process I am providing below has
been developed through experimentation and is based on
several hundred successful Lean programmes in healthcare and
manufacturing organisations.

The approach I will outline is summarised using the acronym
PRISM (standing for Prepare, Roadmap, Implement, Sustain and
Maintain), which is shown diagrammatically below and in detail
later in this chapter.

Going Lean Step 1: Prepare for Lean (PREPARE)

Prior to any actual implementation activity it is essential that
organisations prepare themselves effectively. There are four
activities that need to be considered prior to starting your Lean
programme and these are:

1. **Scoping the Problem** – be clear about the problem you
   are trying to solve, including what you expect to be
   different/better at the end of the process.

2. **Identifying Sponsors & Change Agents** – who will
champion the programme and who will lead/undertake
the actual improvements?

3. **Prepare a Communications Plan** – communicate your
plans and allow people to comment on the process.

4. **Gathering Information** – gather real facts about the
process including baseline data against anything you
want to change.

Some of the key things you might want to do to be clear
about the problem can be undertaken during a 'Scoping
Session' where you will probably want to answer the following
questions:

○ **What are the boundaries?** – Identify the start/end of the
process. For example, are you only looking at the process
inside the organisation or across the whole health
economy?

○ **Why is this project important?** – A statement outlining
why this project is more important than anything
else that those involved could be doing, and what
the expected benefits will be, will help to engage the
participants in the process. This is about creating a
compelling need for Lean or, using a common phrase,
creating a 'burning platform'.

○ **How will we measure success?** – How will you know
when you have achieved what you are looking to
achieve? It is important at this stage to be specific. For
example, 'improved performance' is not a good measure

as it is not as specific as 'improving the number of patients seen by 15%'.

○ **Who needs to involved?** – What specialties and people need to be involved in the Lean programme and who will need to be engaged?

○ **What things don't we want to change (or can't we change)?** – What are the things you don't want to change or accidentally introduce and what things are you not able to change?

○ **What risks and other issues do we need to consider?** – In undertaking this programme what other things do you need to be aware of (such as new procedures, best practice guidance, etc.) and what things may go wrong?

○ **Who will play the key roles in our programme?** – There are a range of key roles that need to be identified as part of the Lean programme and the most important ones are:

  ➤ **Improvement Sponsor/s** – Who will champion the programme from a senior perspective (both clinical and managerial)?

  ➤ **Change Agents** – Who will lead the Lean programme?

  ➤ **Pathway/Process Managers** – Who are the managers who will be essential in helping sell this programme and ensure it is a success?

○ **When will it start and what will happen?** – This is about setting out a plan of action and a timescale plan.

○ **How will we communicate with our team?** – This is about the framework you will establish for communicating with your team and for getting their feedback, including how frequently you communicate, what format it will be in and how you will deal with questions and feedback.

An example guide for running a Scoping Session is shown in Appendix 4.

Apart from being clear about the problem and how you are going to tackle it, which you will address through a Scoping Session, you will also need to consider the development of your team to support the Lean programme. During this process you will need to consider four groups of people as detailed below:

Lean Leaders – those who will lead your Lean programme and will need to have the skills to train others.

Lean Practitioners – those with the ability to initiate projects and improvement activities.

Lean Participants – those with the skills required to allow them to participate in Lean Events.

Lean Aware – everyone else should have a basic understanding of what Lean is and what is going on.

The skills required by each of these four groups are summarised below.

○ **Leaders** need to be able to train others and have

probably been involved in around 40 or more Lean projects.

- ⟡ **Practitioners** should have all the skills to initiate and run successful Lean projects and to facilitate groups and teams.

- ⟡ **Participants** need to have the essential skills to enable them to successfully participate in Lean Events.

- ⟡ Those who only need to be **Lean Aware** must understand the basics of Lean and what is going on, as well as how they can find out more and what (if any) contribution they can make to the programme.

Further details of the skills required by each group are detailed in Appendix 8.

Going Lean Step 2: Set out a Roadmap (ROADMAP)

Having prepared your organisation for Lean, you will need a Roadmap of how you will get from where you are (what is called Current State or 'As Is') to where you want to go to (called Future State or 'To Be').

The basic tool used by organisations during this phase is Value Stream Mapping and that is what I will focus on here. Value Stream Mapping is a creative process that aims to change the way that people think about how they deliver services currently and enables participants to create a solution that is closest to being 'optimal' (in Lean terms this means being closest to eliminating all Non-Value Adding activities but also has the minimum patient safety risk exposure).

Value Stream Mapping is normally used to redesign big processes, such as the end-to-end clinical pathway for gastroenterology, for example, from initial referral until the patient is safely home after surgery, and may therefore involve people from three or more organisations and many different professions or areas of expertise. If you do not look at the end-to-end process there is a chance that you will design a solution that has built in problems and that just transfers risk and costs elsewhere in the pathway.

For smaller processes (such as how a single GP Practice works or the activities in a pathology lab), Value Stream Mapping might be a bit of an overkill, and there are better techniques we refer to later in this book that are more suited to such situations.

The three steps in Value Stream Mapping are normally described as:

1. **Understand the Current State** – this is about understanding how you currently deliver services and is an important step on the basis most people know their own role well but often only vaguely understand what goes on elsewhere in the process.

2. **Create a 'Blue Sky' Vision** – this creative process is about getting the team to design an 'ideal' solution assuming they could do anything. This is designed to create a list of great ideas that can be used during the third step below.

3. **Design a realistic 'Future State'** – using the ideas generated throughout the first two steps, this is about creating a realistic 'Future State' that defines how the process will operate in the future (normally it is set 6–18 months in the future) and then to define the individual steps that will enable you to get from the Current State to the Future State.

The three steps involved in designing a realistic Future State are shown diagrammatically below. In Lean terms, the Future State is often referred to as 'True North' – being the direction that the organisation should head toward.

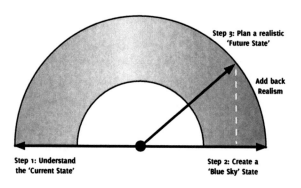

A checklist that can be used to help you plan your Value Stream Mapping event is shown in Appendix 5.

Going Lean Step 3:
Implement the Changes (IMPLEMENTATION)

The third step to consider when going Lean is the implementation process where you convert the plans created in your Future State into tangible improvements. The two most common implementation approaches used in Lean during this phase are Rapid Improvement Events (which are also called Lean Events, Kaizen Events, Kaizen Blitzes, and Rapid Improvement Workshops, etc.) and 2P events (also called Rapid Planning Events) and I have focused predominantly on these types of implementation activities.

Rapid Improvement Events (RIE)

A Rapid Improvement Event (RIE) is a process designed to physically transform a process in a structured manner. The way to think of an RIE is that if a process can be transformed by getting a group of 5–30 people together for 1–5 days then that is a Rapid Improvement Event. Examples of successful RIEs include:

- Tackling patient flow and drug management in A&E

- Improving the flow and Utilisation of Pre-Assessment

- Reducing the number of delayed transfers of care across a local health economy

- Reducing falls for patients in secondary care

- Improving the safety and productivity of staff on wards

- Improving adherence to start times and introducing pull in theatres

- Improving the effectiveness of pharmacy promotion campaigns in primary care

- Improving the take up of breast screening services

A detailed checklist for a Rapid Improvement Event is shown in Appendix 6 and the tools you might use during one are described in Chapter 6. The key point about Rapid Improvement Events is that they are used to make changes happen and are not purely 'planning' processes. There is some confusion about this point and also around the duration of them with some people thinking that they must be five days long irrespective of whether they need to be or not. The reality is Rapid Improvement Events only need to be as long as they need to be and you should not artificially drag them out as that is the way to disengage your front-line staff.

2P (aka Rapid Planning Events)

Some processes are too high risk to move straight to a Rapid Improvement Event. A 2P (Process Planning) event is used to de-risk critical processes prior to implementing the changes. You can either use a 2P event as a surrogate Value Stream Mapping event for smaller processes (remembering that Value Stream Mapping is a bit of an overkill for smaller processes), or as an intermediate event between a Value Stream Mapping event and a Rapid Improvement Event where the risk is high.

Example 2P events include:

- Planning theatre lists and scheduling

- Complex discharge planning

- Planning a reduction in medication risk

- Planning a 'one stop shop' in outpatients

- Integrating alcohol pathways into a drug treatment pathway

- Improving the utilisation of rehabilitation beds

- Establishing dedicated recovery facilities

Like a Rapid Improvement Event, a 2P event will last for between one and five days (again depending on the process to be covered). The output of a 2P event is normally a detailed implementation plan, layout and risk review for the new process, and they are normally followed by one or more RIEs where the physical changes are implemented.

2P events follow a similar process to that of a Value Stream Mapping (VSM) event, and the example checklist for the VSM event given in Appendix 5 can be used to cover a 2P event as well.

Going Lean Step 4: Sustain the Changes (SUSTAIN)

Strangely, more benefit is often realised after the Rapid Improvement Events than during it. For a healthcare organisation to realise these benefits they must focus not only on changing processes but also on changing behaviours and establishing a process for continuously improving. This section outlines some of the key steps that can be taken to ensure you sustain the change.

Managing for Daily Improvement

Managing for Daily Improvement is about getting the team together quickly every day to discuss issues, actions and further improvements. It will need some support to avoid it becoming a moans and groans session and lots of management support to ensure it happens, but it will reinforce the new process and also facilitate continuous improvement.

Management Audits

In addition to a focus on daily improvements, managers play a big role in embedding the improvements and this is best achieved by active participation in management audits of the process. This can be based around the 5S Audit shown in Appendix 2 (and we will cover 5S later) or via a daily review of any outstanding actions that are left over from the Rapid Improvement Event. Sometimes, just being present will do and 'Management By Walking About' (MBWA) is a well-established process for helping managers to engage with their teams and remain close to the problems they are encountering.

Communication & Coaching

Frequent communication about the progress of your programme and results to date as well as allowing people to contribute to further improvements and giving them support/time to deal with any issues or concerns that arise, is an excellent way of involving and motivating people.

Going Lean Step 5: Maintain the Momentum (MAINTAIN)

The fifth and final step in going Lean is to consider how you will maintain the momentum of improvement. The simplest way to ensure you maintain the momentum is to go back to the beginning and start again!

However you decide to proceed after your first round of improvement activities, you will need to know what the real journey to Lean feels like and I have shown this in the diagram below.

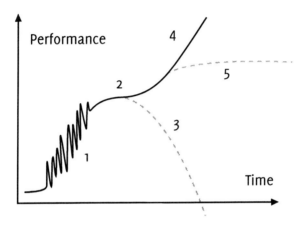

There are five numbered events to be aware of as shown in the diagram above and these are:

1. After an initial start up that will normally involve scoping the problem and at least one Value Stream Mapping event, the organisation will get into the process of actually implementing Lean. This feels very bumpy as assumptions are challenged and some things go better than others. At this stage someone will go to your boss and complain about what has gone on so far. This is the first crisis point and many organisations will have a 'Crisis of Confidence' resulting in the programme stalling.

2. After a while (sometimes after quite a few months), the noise will reduce and it will feel like the process is

slowing down – but in reality it is just becoming 'the way things are done' as improved processes finally become changed behaviours and this is when you will start to realise the full benefits of your Lean improvement.

3. It is at this stage when the organisation thinks it has 'gone Lean' that a second crisis point arises, namely the crisis of 'Process v Behavioural Change'. The focus will switch to the next problem before the behavioural change has really bedded in and this results in the performance dropping as the old ways of doing things and the old bad practices start to slip back in.

4. Assuming you have avoided the first and second crisis points, and having reached a new level of working, you will find performance again starts to accelerate.

5. At this point organisations often encounter a third crisis point, namely the crisis of 'Lean Programme v Lean Cultural Change'. This is reached when they decide to end their 'Lean Programme'. Referring back to the fifth Lean principle (Perfection), Lean can be shown to be a journey. Those organisations who treat it as a programme will find that the gains they have made will slip away, sometimes this will occur slowly and sometimes very quickly, unless the organisation continues to improve and 'go Lean'.

| **Prepare** for Lean | Set out a **Roadmap** | **Implement** the Changes | **Sustain** the Changes | **Maintain** the Momentum |

In closing this chapter, I will remind you of my comment from the first chapter that Lean was simply structured common sense. The key word in this statement was that it needs a structure to be successful. The five-stage structure we have looked at provides you with the basic framework and in the following chapters we will look at some of the tools and concepts that underpin it.

Chapter 3 Self Assessment Questions

• Name the three typical crisis points reached in a
  Lean programme

• What does the acronym PRISM stand for?

• Describe the three steps in Value Stream Mapping

• What is the difference between a Rapid Improvement Event
  and a 2P event?

Chapter 4

Lean at different organisational levels

Where do you start with Lean in your organisation? Do you want to change your entire organisation or just a single reception desk? Are you going for 'Global Lean Leadership' in healthcare or 'Local Improvement'? Your answers to these questions will determine how you structure your Lean programme and in this section we look at three possible starting points:

- **Organisation Wide** – introducing Lean across your entire organisation

- **Pathway Level** – introducing Lean across one or more pathways or Value Streams such as the end-to-end neurology pathway or in emergency care

- **Process Level** – introducing Lean in one or more areas such as the pathology lab or finance

Each level has its associated positives and negatives and in this section I will introduce what each means and why organisations choose to start at that point.

Level 1: Organisation Wide

The highest level at which Lean can be introduced is at the Organisation level, which is sometimes referred to as 'Enterprise Level'. This is where an organisation looks to go Lean across all functions and in all areas, and is normally driven by a very strong desire to change the organisational culture and to become best in class for one or more specialties. The benefits for those organisations with the tenacity to achieve this are enormous, but because of the time investment required (and sometimes the risk of doing it) few organisations are ready to take the plunge at this level.

Positives	Negatives
○ Drives a change in the way the organisation behaves	○ Requires long-term commitment from the senior team
○ High levels of performance improvement achieved	○ Can be easily derailed by senior opponents, especially in the early days
○ Very motivating for staff who are involved in the process	○ Requires good relationships across the local health economy for an extended period of time

Level 2: Pathway Level

This level focuses on introducing Lean across one or more end-to-end pathways. This is by far the most common starting point for organisations as it still has a big impact but is not as resource intensive or disruptive as going for the whole Organisation Wide change. Also, starting at the Pathway Level is more likely to avoid the risks associated with introducing improvements at the 'Process Level' that we cover next. Even those organisations that go on to introduce Lean across their entire organisation will often have started at this level with pilot programmes to prove the concepts.

Positives	Negatives
○ Results are seen more quickly than in the Organisation Wide level	○ Still requires a lot of management input and good relations across the local health economy
○ Less resource intensive than Organisation Wide level	○ Can result in islands of excellence in the organisation that eventually get worn down by the inefficiencies in other areas and processes
○ Less prone to creating upstream or downstream risks than the process level because of its end-to-end focus	○ Is prone to having an 'end date' to solve a specific issue rather than being about fundamental and long-term change in the way services are delivered
○ Can be used to 'prove' the concept prior to implementation across the organisation	

Level 3: Process Level

At this level the introduction of Lean is normally about fixing problems in a single department or area. It is quick and easy to introduce the changes as you normally only have to deal with one or a few departments and teams. However, at this level you are making improvements in isolation and there is a big risk you will simply transfer risk and cost elsewhere in the organisation or pathway. Because you will also be creating a small 'island of excellence' it is likely that the benefits you achieve will simply get swamped by problems elsewhere in the organisation.

To show how this might happen imagine an emergency care pathway involving A&E, a Medical Assessment Unit (MAU) and various other areas as shown conceptually in the diagram on the next page.

At the Process Level we might wish to only make improvements within MAU, perhaps around how they accept patients from A&E and how they eventually transfer the patient to the wards, but by only looking at the MAU process it is possible that A&E will find it harder to transfer patients into MAU, and the wards may find that when they receive patients they do not have the right information to create an effective discharge plan (again this is only an example).

The net effect of this change in MAU could be that A&E decide to change the process of transferring patients that forces MAU to accept them, and that the wards introduce a system whereby they will refuse to accept the transfer of care until the information is available in a format they can use to help them with discharge planning. Now this may appear speculative but in reality it is what happens when healthcare organisations choose to make isolated improvements at the Process Level and not unsurprisingly the negatives for starting at this level often outweigh the positives.

Positives	Negatives
◗ Very quick to implement changes ◗ Minimal disruption to the organisation ◗ Least amount of resources used of the three levels ◗ Useful for very small scale issues	◗ Often leads to fragmented improvements and the transfer of risk and costs elsewhere in the pathway ◗ Little or no impact on the wider organisation ◗ Liable to being swamped by the backlash from other areas or simply worn away by the process rubbing up against non-Lean processes ◗ Difficult to move on from this level to the Pathway Level as it normally requires you to 'undo' the changes that were made at the Process Level ◗ Normally have difficulty in engaging senior management as the results are very localised

In addition to the three most common starting points or levels I have focused on here, there are two additional starting points you may consider. The first is the 'health economy level' that looks at all specialities and all services across all agencies. The second is the 'function' level, such as looking at 'all theatres' or 'all district nursing teams' to share learning. At the health economy level the need for coordination across organisations is very high and outside of the scope of this introductory text. At the function level, you normally need to have done some pilot projects and activities before you consider this starting point. Function level projects suffer from many of the same issues as a Process Level start but require more coordination, with the benefit being shared learning across the function. Again, starting at the function level is beyond the scope of this introductory text.

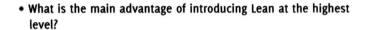

Chapter 4 Self Assessment Questions

• What are the three most common levels at which you can introduce Lean?

• What is the main advantage of introducing Lean at the highest level?

• What are the benefits of introducing Lean at the lowest level?

• Why do most people 'going Lean' start at the middle level?

Chapter 5

Thinking Lean

This chapter introduces further Lean terminology and concepts that you will find invaluable when dealing with teams involved in Lean activities. These concepts help groups to think about the issues without them getting distracted by minor issues at the expense of the big picture.

Planned & Emergent Work

In Lean terminology, activity that can be predicted is called **'Planned Work'** and activity that cannot be planned is called **'Emergent Work'**.

Planned Work normally includes things you can put in your diary, such as clinics, theatre sessions, reporting, meetings, etc.

Emergent Work is work that 'emerges' and cannot be planned and includes such things as power cuts, dealing with major incidents and 'snap' performance audits.

Adding together all the work you can Plan and all the work that Emerges gives you the total demand for work to be done in a process.

Now a basic assumption is that you can only improve the things you can plan and you have to build in an allowance for emergent work, maybe as a safety factor. You will get questions from the front-line teams about what happens if the process they are designing goes wrong (for example, a patient who collapses during an outpatient session) and this is where building a safety factor into the process is useful.

Having said that, some things that appear emergent can actually be planned. The most common examples are in Emergency Care where it may be impossible to know what the symptoms of the next patient who presents will be, but you can look at trends and patterns to work out the average and peak demand for care over previous weeks and months and ensure you have the capacity to manage that demand, plus a safety factor for any incidents that arise, with the size of the safety factor increasing as the uncertainty about the required demand increases.

The key for teams is to focus on improving the things you can plan for and build in contingency for what you can't.

Runner, Repeater & Stranger

Another important Lean idea that we have already encountered is the frequency of different types of activity, such as the frequency with which patients present with certain conditions. These conditions can be broken down into Runners, Repeaters and Strangers.

- A **Runner** is an activity or condition that is an everyday (or sometimes many times per day) occurrence and is very familiar to the team.

- A **Repeater** is something that occurs less regularly, maybe only a few times per week or month, but the team is still familiar with the condition or issue.

○ A **Stranger** is something that occurs only rarely (say, less frequently than once per month) and normally causes the team to have to stop and think about how to deal with the situation.

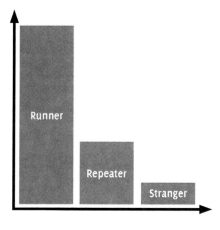

I am yet to find a healthcare organisation or clinical specialty that does not meet the rule of thumb that there are many different types of Strangers but collectively they make up only a small percentage of the work done compared to the few types of Runners and Repeaters that make up the bulk of the work.

The focus of Lean should be on designing a process that optimises the work done for Runners and Repeaters (as this will yield the best return), but which can accommodate Strangers when they arise. The reality is that there are normally so many Strangers that could arise that it would be impossible to design a process that was optimised for every single condition, and it is better to improve the bulk of the work done as overall you will have more time to deal with the Strangers if and when they arise.

Takt Time

Takt Time is a very important concept in Lean as it defines the 'beat rate' of a process, meaning the frequency that a 'customer' demands something from the process, such as the frequency of patients arriving at a clinic or the frequency of invoices being received by a finance department.

It is calculated as follows: **Available Time/Demand Rate**

An example Takt Time calculation is shown below:

The A&E Department is open 24 hours per day (1440 minutes) and in that time will deal with (on average) 480 people. The Takt Time is therefore: 1440/480 = 3 minutes. This means that 'On Average' the process is triggered every 3 minutes by the arrival of a patient.

Obviously, you would need to be clear about the levels of variation over the time period chosen in the calculation, but as a starting point for working out the demand for a service, Takt Time is a very useful concept.

Manual Cycle Time and Lead Time

Lead Time is the elapsed time from the start till the end of a process (Clock Start to Clock Stop).

Manual Cycle Time (also referred to as Process Time or even Touch Time) is the amount of work that is done during the elapsed time.

The difference between Lead Time and Manual Cycle Time is shown diagrammatically on the next page.

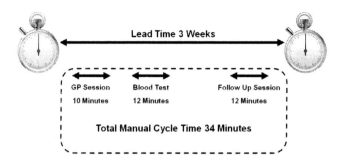

Using the total Manual Cycle Time for a process and the Takt Time discussed earlier you can make a very basic assessment of the minimum number of staff required to run a process as shown in the following example.

Using the Takt Time of 3 minutes calculated earlier and using an assumption that every patient needs an average of 30 minutes of care (spread across receptionists, nurses, doctors, etc.) in A&E we can calculate the minimum headcount from the equation Manual Cycle Time/Takt Time, namely 30 minutes/ 3 minutes = 10 people. Therefore, the minimum number of staff required to run this process is 10.

We can use the same equation (MCT/Takt Time) to break this down by staff groups so that we can tell exactly how many staff of each specialism we would require to run the process.

This is a calculation for minimum headcount and does not take into account any safety factors for Emergent Work and we may have to look at the process in smaller time chunks to get a more realistic staffing plan (for example we may see spikes in demand on Friday evening or Monday morning), but as a rule of thumb this is a very useful calculation to be able to use.

'5 Second Rule'

Put simply, the 5 Second Rule means: **"An informed person walking into an area should be able to know enough about the process to remain safe, know where things are and to understand what is happening in less than 5 seconds"**

How often do people come into the office, ward or department and spend a long time trying to determine what the current status is? Whether that is the backlog of calls, the availability of swabs or the location of staff, it is often a very large percentage of the total working day. This is very wasteful of resources and leads to numerous errors and mistakes and the aim of the '5 Second Rule' is to create an environment where problems can be quickly seen without tying up large amounts of time and resource.

Going to Gemba

Gemba is a Japanese word used to mean 'the place where work is done' (but literally translating as 'the actual place'). An important concept when undertaking Lean activities is to 'Walk the Process', and 'Going to Gemba' (meaning to go to the place where work is done and see what really happens) allows you to see exactly what happens and to avoid the pitfall of 'guessing'.

Chapter 5 Self Assessment Questions

- What is the calculation for Takt Time?

- What does MCT stand for?

- How can MCT and Takt Time help you calculate minimum staffing?

- Define Gemba

Chapter 6

The Key Lean Tools

In this section I introduce the Top 5 Lean Tools that I believe will deliver the biggest benefit for healthcare organisations. In addition, I have used this chapter to also provide a brief introduction to some of the other tools that you may come across on your journey to Lean. All of the five key tools are implementation tools and are commonly used during Rapid Improvement Events.

Key Tool 1: 5S

5S is a tool designed to create a 'Visual Workplace'. A Visual Workplace is one where things are organised logically and that maximises productivity as this reduces time spent searching and also reduces a wide range of risks from slips, trips and falls to the risk of running out of essential drugs. A Visual Workplace will also conform to the '5 Second Rule' mentioned earlier.

5S is often confused by some people as being a 'tidy up' but in fact it is a systematic way of managing a process to improve productivity (by making easier to find equipment, consumables, information, etc.) and reduce risk to staff and patients.

5S originally came from five Japanese words that began with a sound similar to S in English. These original words have been changed to five equivalent words in English. The words used sometimes vary (for example, some people use Sweep in place of

Shine) but the most commonly used list of words is shown below:

- **Sort** – remove unwanted items from the area to reduce clutter

- **Set** – set what remains in order and give each item a marked 'home location'

- **Shine** – keep the area clean and return items to their 'home location' at the ends of shifts etc.

- **Standardise** – define the responsibilities of Teams & Managers in maintaining standards

- **Sustain** – audit and improve the area

Expanding these summary descriptions we get a five-step process to creating a Visual Workplace as described below:

Step 1: Sort

The first of the 5Ss is concerned with removing unwanted items from an area. This often involves what is called a 'Red Tag Attack' that involves touching every item in an area (and the touching part is important when you realise that people stop seeing clutter and mess after it has been in place for as little as two days) and determining whether or not the item is in use and required. If it is not in use, and is not a safety critical item, or is not required, then it should be removed from the area and put into a 'Red Tag Area', with the term Red Tag being from the days when people tagged faulty or unwanted items with a literal red tag. After a while items in the Red Tag Area will either need to be returned (because they are in fact required), transferred or disposed of.

Step 2: Set

Having removed the unused or unwanted items, Set is about giving all the things that are required a logical home, and it is at this stage people consider marking floors, desks, shelves, etc. and giving items marked homes. If appropriate, you can go further, for example by designing shaped trays with 'cut-outs' for equipment to fit into that quickly show what is missing from the box by the resultant empty space. However, with increased intensity comes increased costs of implementing Set and you will need to decide how far to take it.

Step 3: Shine

The third step is concerned with two things" making less mess and ensuring things are put back at the end of a shift or day.

Step 4: Standardise

The fourth step is about ensuring that everyone understands the process, it is standardised as far as possible across the team and the process for managing 5S is documented.

Step 5: Sustain

The fifth step is concerned with ensuring that the other four steps 'stick' (which is the alternative name you will sometimes read in place of sustain) and the basis of this are audits and management involvement to stop old bad habits slipping back in. In Appendix 2 I have provided a simple 5S Audit form to use during this phase.

Closing Points

5S is a robust and widely used implementation tool. Sometimes people will refer to a sixth S, namely 'Safety', but in reality you should be thinking about safety at every step in the process rather than as a separate step in its own right.

Key Tool 2: Standard Work

At its simplest, Standard Work is a tool for ensuring that everyone follows the 'most effective' and 'least waste' process based on the available equipment, people and other resources. Concepts we have already come across such as Takt Time and Manual Cycle Time are integral to our understanding of designing a 'least waste' process and Standard Work. The key words in this paragraph are that Standard Work is based on the 'available equipment, people and other resources' and it does not specifically mean that there is a need to buy expensive new equipment or hire new staff to achieve a 'standard' process.

Other examples of Standard Work concepts include the following:

Method Sheets

These are documents that detail how a process will be carried out. Healthcare organisations are generally full of such documents that can be variously called 'Standard Operating Procedures', 'Clinical Procedures' or 'Work Instructions' and these normally look either like large reports or simplified flow charts. True Method Sheets for a Lean project detail the activities that are actually happening not just the key steps. For example, it is possible to show the flowchart for a shift handover in two or three steps but in reality there is normally a lot more to it than the summary flowchart would indicate.

Layout Sheets

A new process will often require a detailed plan of how the area is laid out and indicating where potential safety hazards can be found as shown in the example below. Standard Work Layout Charts help with identifying where things should be located as part of your 5S exercise.

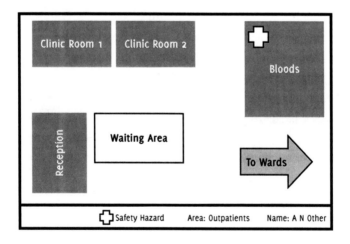

Loading Charts

These charts are used to show how the work is broken down between individuals and to identify any bottlenecks and minimum staffing as shown overleaf.

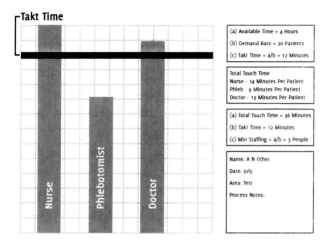

What this Loading Chart shows is that, assuming a patient presents on average every 12 minutes, the Nurse (who on average requires 14 minutes with a patient) will never be able to keep up, the Phlebotomist will be waiting between every patient for the next one to arrive, and then there will be a further queue waiting for the Doctor who will fall behind by 1 minute for every patient who presents in this scenario.

This is a very simplified example to show how a Loading Chart might be used in a real situation and how it can highlight bottlenecks and issues.

Key Points Sheet

A Key Points Sheet is used to highlight a single important issue that you want people to be aware of. An example is shown opposite.

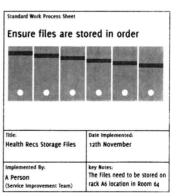

Leader Standard Work

A further concept of Standard Work is to have Leader Standard Work that defines how the Leader of the area/team/department etc. will manage their process. Good Leader Standard Work will detail how problems and issues should be identified and tackled, how often audits will be undertaken and the other steps that will be taken to ensure that the improvements achieved can be sustained.

Key Tool 3: Flow

We have already encountered flow earlier in this book when we covered the '5 Principles of Lean'. Flow is concerned with eliminating delays between stages and enabling processes to achieve 'One Piece Flow' as shown in the following example.

The diagram shown has a 'batch' process where 10 items need to be processed through four Steps (A, B, C & D). All 10 items are done at Step A before being passed to Step B where all 10 are done before being passed on, and so on.

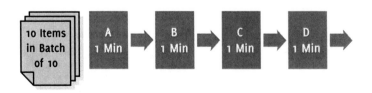

The impact of this 'batching' is that the first item is not received out of Step D until 31 minutes after the start of the process and the last arrives 40 minutes after the start of the process.

If we contrast this with a process that 'Flows' (technically called One Piece Flow), where items are passed 'one at a time' from Step A to Step B and so on as shown below, we see a remarkable change in the overall Lead Time of the process.

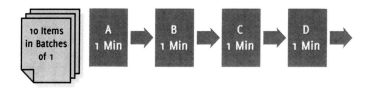

The first item is received out from Step D in 4 minutes and the last in 13 minutes, a reduction of over 66% when compared against the Lead Time in the 'batch' example.

Making a process 'Flow' is about removing barriers between steps (physical, cultural, etc.), moving steps closer together and setting up each step so that it can perform its task without stopping by having the right equipment in the right place (or easily accessible) and people who are properly trained to run a consistent and standard process.

Key Tool 4: Pull

We have already encountered this when we reviewed the five Lean Principles earlier and a 'Pull' System (also called a Kanban system, with Kanban meaning 'signal' or 'ticket' in Japanese) is a system that triggers activity 'on demand' – with the aim of ensuring that work is not done before it is required and that it occurs at the right time to ensure the process keeps 'flowing'.

Pull systems can be used to improve the 'flow' of patients through theatres, improving the utilisation of staff and reducing overall patient lead times, but it can also be used to control consumables so that the team never run out of basic consumables and can also be used to trigger the generation of paperwork etc.

I will use two very simple real-life examples to illustrate 'Pull' further:

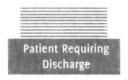

In the first example, the arrival of a set of patient notes in the tray triggers either a junior doctor or a medical secretary to type a discharge letter and give it to the patient. In the real-life scenario this is taken from, it reduced the overall lead time to produce the discharge letter from more than 20 days to less than 1 hour.

In the second example I have shown what is called a

'two bin pull system' where items are stored in two different coloured bins (or storage containers). When the first (darker) container becomes empty it is removed to an area to be refilled and this exposes the lighter coloured container. The difference in colour makes it immediately obvious that the darker container is missing and needs to be refilled. A second benefit of having the second (lighter coloured) container is that the team still have not completely 'run out' of materials and, assuming that they do not use items more quickly than the darker bin is refilled then they will not run out. Obviously the quantity required in each bin needs to be set to a level that accounts for the frequency of use of the items multiplied by the time taken to refill the container. For example, if the team use 20 per day and the container can be refilled in three days you will need a minimum of 60 items. It is normal to add a quantity to this amount for 'safety' and to cope with any peaks in demand.

A 'two bin pull system' may seem a small improvement but in one real-life example a team released the equivalent of two people's worth of time back to giving care by eliminating the time spent constantly looking for items, equipment and consumables.

Key Tool 5: Poka Yoke (Mistake Proofing)

The last of the five key tools I believe will make the biggest difference to healthcare organisations is Poka Yoke. This translates literally from Japanese as 'Errors Avoid'. The most common English translation is the term Mistake Proofing, and it describes the process of designing out problems and issues and trying to prevent human error or other risks from arising in the first place.

The classic example of a 'Mistake Proof' solution that people in the UK will be familiar with is of a three-pin electric plug. There is no way that a normal user can insert the plug into a socket in any other way than the correct way (without a mallet) and it is therefore 'Mistake Proof' against incorrect fitting. In addition, the need to wire up plugs on electrical goods purchased in the UK has been changed by having the plug pre-fitted and tested so that the risk of incorrect wiring has been eliminated.

Not all problems can be made 'Mistake Proof' so effectively and there is a hierarchy of improvement with varying degrees of effectiveness that is shown below:

- **Eliminate** the problem by designing out the problem/ step/process

- If you can't eliminate it, can you **Replace** it by installing a safer process/step?

- If you can't replace it, can you **Redesign** it to reduce the risk of problems arising?

- If you can't redesign it, can you **Reduce** the risk of it going wrong?

- If you can't reduce the risk, can you **Detect** the problem more quickly?

- If you can't detect the problem, can you **Mitigate** the impact of any occurrences of the problem?

I have shown below a common example for each of the six levels of Mistake Proofing:

- **Eliminate** – Electrical goods being supplied ready fitted with a 3-pin plug has eliminated the risk of accidentally wiring the plug up incorrectly.

- **Replace** – The old process of checking train tickets by hand is being replaced by an automatic ticket checker that reduces the risk of people getting through without paying.

○ **Redesign** – Lawn mowers have been redesigned to incorporate 'cut-outs' and earth leakage circuit breakers to reduce the risk of electrocution if the cables are cut and also reduces the risk of the mower running on, and the mower causing damage if the user loses control of it, by cutting the power off when a cut-out switch is released.

○ **Reduce** – Traffic lights are designed to reduce the risk of people crashing at junctions and the risk of traffic jams.

○ **Detect** – Tyre pressure monitors on cars are designed to detect a sudden or slow leak and therefore reduce the risk of a 'blow out' or a flat tyre and the corresponding damage it causes.

○ **Mitigate** – Airbags in cars are designed to reduce (or mitigate) the damage caused by a high speed impact.

There are many examples of Mistake Proofing in healthcare, from limits on the opening of windows to controls on drugs to prevent errors, but there are generally many other improvements that can be made. Next time something goes wrong, from a patient turning up at the wrong reception through to something more serious, the thought should always be on 'how can we redesign the process to avoid this problem occurring again?'

Other Tools of Lean

Although the majority of Lean improvements in healthcare will be based on the key five tools above, it is important that Lean Practitioners are aware of some of the other tools and concepts that underpin Lean improvements.

TPM (Total Productive Maintenance)

TPM (Total Productive Maintenance) is a concept whereby front-line teams are given responsibility for day- to-day servicing of the processes/equipment they use (which itself is called Autonomous Maintenance). The principle is that empowering front-line teams to manage the routine 'servicing' of their process frees time from other professionals and managers and reduces the number of occasions when the process/equipment fails completely.

TPM has application in all healthcare processes where the process is dependent on key equipment that, if faulty, can stop the process because of a lack of alternative facilities.

SMED (Single Minute Exchange of Die) – also known as Set-Up Reduction

The concept of SMED is that it should never take longer than 9 minutes (hence Single Minute) to change over from one activity to the next, whether that is the time from the end of one operation to the start of the next, or the end of one clinic appointment to the start of the next.

The standard analogy of how you achieve this reduction in changeover times is to compare the changing of tyres in Formula 1 racing with doing it at home, and I have shown this below.

Example of home changeover:	Example of Formula 1 changeover:
○ Search for car keys	○ Inform 'pit team' you are 'coming in'
○ Try to dig out jack, tools etc from garage	○ Park in marked area
○ Read manual to determine where to put jack	○ Slide under jack and raise car
○ Read manual to check how to remove wheel	○ Release wheel nuts (1 per wheel)
○ Find wheel locking nut in glove box	○ Put on new wheels
○ Have a cup of tea	○ Drop car back onto ground
○ Locate jack and pump up car	○ Drive away
○ Struggle to remove wheel nuts	
○ Remove old wheel and fit new wheel	
○ Struggle to lock wheel nuts again	
○ Lower car	
Total Elapsed Time: 1 Hour?	Total Elapsed Time: 8 Seconds

The difference in Formula 1 is that they have got all the equipment in place prior to the car coming into the pits, they have designed the process to make it easy to remove the wheels, the team have trained to work together and the process has been standardised to make it easy to follow for everyone and reduce both risk and time.

Set-Up Reduction (SMED) has extensive application in theatres, clinics and labs.

Heijunka

Heijunka is used to 'level' the activity in a process to avoid peaks and troughs are far as possible. Heijunka has lots of useful applications within healthcare environments from reducing mix and volume variation in clinics to managing peaks and troughs in pathology.

String Diagram (aka Spaghetti Diagrams)

This is an extremely useful tool for mapping how people and information move around an area. The idea is to imagine a person walking around dragging 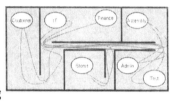 their feet which in turn are covered in paint and you will create a picture like the one opposite.

FMEA (Failure Modes & Effects Analysis)

FMEA (Failure Modes & Effects Analysis) creates a priority list for addressing risks/issues in a process by multiplying level of risk. An example FMEA Form is shown in Appendix 3.

Backbone & Ribs (aka Seven Flows)

Backbone and Ribs is a tool normally used during a Rapid Planning Event (RPE). The Backbone of the process is shown running down the middle of the diagram. At right angles to each step are the six ribs that detail what needs to be in place to enable the step to work effectively. A representation of a Backbone & Ribs is shown on the next page:

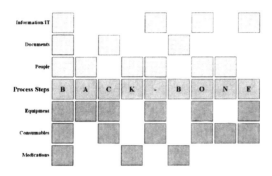

Backbone and Ribs is a very important planning tool that can avoid unexpected surprises during implementation.

Try Its

Also known as 'Cardboard Engineering', a 'Try It' exercise involves using full sized models (often cut from cardboard) to identify whether items/equipment will fit prior to installing them and to identify any problems that might be incurred during the implementation process.

5 Whys (Root Cause Analysis)

5 Whys is a simple tool used to help identify the root cause of a problem. It relies on asking the question 'Why?' five times, with the idea being that the root cause will be exposed by the time of the fifth question as shown on the next page:

Problem: Patient Not Called As Promised

- **Why 1** - Why did the Patient not get called back?
  Answer 1 – Because they did not appear on the 'to call' list

- **Why 2** - Why did their name not appear on the 'to call' list?
  Answer 2 – Because their details were not in the folder

- **Why 3** - Why were their details not in the folder?
  Answer 3 – Because the person doing it did not use the standard checklist

- **Why 4** - Why was the standard checklist not used?
  Answer 4 – Because person X had not been inducted and therefore didn't know about it

- **Why 5** - Why did we not induct 'X' correctly?
  (Root Cause)

Pareto Analysis

Pareto Analysis is a technique that works on the 80/20 rule which is an assumption that 80% of the problems/issues are caused by only 20% of the causes or activities. The aim of Pareto Analysis is to identify the 'critical few' issues that are causing the majority of problems and to tackle these issues first.

SPC (Statistical Process Control)

SPC (Statistical Process Control) is a tool frequently used in Lean and Six Sigma projects to monitor the performance of a process, to measure variance and to spot trends that could indicate a problem or dangerous activity prior to it occurring.

Fishbone Diagrams (Ishikawa Diagrams)

A Fishbone Diagram, which is also known as 'Cause & Effect Diagram', is a creative tool used to identify the primary causes of a problem (effect). The causes are often categorised by the '4Ms' of Materials, Men, Machines and Methods as shown in the diagram.

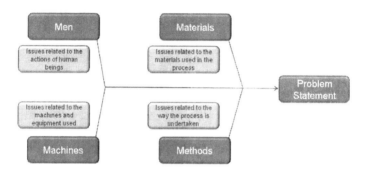

Hand-Off Chart (aka Circle Diagram)

A Hand-Off Chart lists the departments involved in a process and shows how information and customers move around the process. A line is drawn each time a piece of information or a patient is 'handed off' to someone else in the process and the resulting chart is excellent for visually highlighting faulty processes.

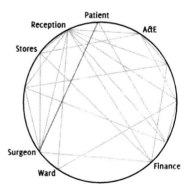

Jidoka (aka Autonomation or the automation of human activity)

Jidoka is often referred to as 'automation with a human face' and is the concept of empowering teams to stop processes when problems/issues arise so that they can be fixed, combined with the selective automation of the process to reduce the risk of problems arising in the first place.

Lean Tools Matrix

In the following table I have attempted to show where each tool might be used as part of either a Value Stream Mapping event, Rapid Improvement Event or Rapid Planning Event as described earlier.

Lean Tool Matrix	Value Stream Mapping	Rapid Improvement Event	Rapid Planning Event
5S		✓	
Standard Work	✓	✓	✓
Flow	✓	✓	
Pull	✓	✓	
Mistake Proofing		✓	
TPM		✓	
SMED	✓	✓	
Heijunka		✓	
FMEA		✓	✓
Backbone & Ribs	✓		✓
Try Its	✓		✓
5 Whys	✓	✓	✓
Pareto Analysis	✓		✓
SPC		✓	
Hand-Off Charts	✓		✓
Jidoka		✓	

Chapter 6 Self Assessment Questions

- What does 5S stand for?

- Name two Standard Work concepts?

- Identify an example of Flow or Pull in your organisation

- Identify an example of Mistake Proofing in your organisation

Chapter 7

The top 8 problems with Lean

In this chapter, I have listed the eight most common problems that Practitioners will find with the implementation of Lean programmes and suggested how you might deal with each issue.

1. Confusing Lean with Process Mapping or other tactical approaches

A lot of your team will have tried Process Mapping (and the resulting tinkering with the process that this leads to without a formal 'Future State') and will think of this as Lean. Once they have experienced a Value Stream Mapping event this perception will go away very quickly, but until then you will have to smile when the team moan that they do not want to do 'process mapping' again.

2. Failing to move from discussion to action

A lot of organisational inertia surrounds previous programmes which failed to move from 'doing improvement on paper' to actually implementing the improvements. Creating some 'quick wins' will overcome this issue very quickly and prove that your Lean programme is not like the things that have gone before.

3. Not dealing with roadblocks effectively

As you progress through your improvement activities you will encounter 'roadblocks', these being things that people put in front of you to prevent the team moving forward, and you will need to spend some time trying to decipher what are real problems that you need to deal with and which are just diversions. There are a couple of useful sayings which might help you in this matter:

- ⭕ **"It is better to achieve 80% now rather than 100% never."** – meaning it is better to implement a solution that makes 80% of occurrences better rather than trying to design a solution that is completely 'ideal' as you will never move from discussion into action if you try to deal with every scenario.

- ⭕ **"Design for the most likely solution and you will have more time to deal with the exceptions."** – This statement suggests you design your process/pathway to operate within the most likely limits or to cope with the most likely maximum and minimum volumes and you will eliminate most of the problems and have much more time to deal with exceptional circumstances.

4. Leading from the Middle

Without the support of a senior level Improvement Sponsor, it can be a waste of your time doing Lean. It is very difficult to implement and almost impossible to sustain improvements without top level support, so treat that as your number one priority. You should also consider how you will 'Manage for Daily Improvement' and this is achieved by your 'Leader

Standard Work' covered earlier. Different levels of Leaders need to undertake specific activities: departmental managers need to manage your Lean performance measures and do regular audits, as well as leading regular continuous improvement sessions, whilst more senior managers need to 'walk the boards and the wards', demonstrating their support for Lean as well as chairing improvement sessions on occasions.

5. Failing to 'Follow Up'

Having implemented changes it is essential to keep some focus on ensuring that the process does not 'slip back' and that team behaviours are changed as well as their processes. This requires regular management input (again Leader Standard Work comes into this) for a number of weeks after the process's changes have been implemented.

6. Failing to deal with the genuine concerns of the team

When a Lean programme is announced everyone will immediately think about 'WIIFM' (What's in it for me?). This does not mean that they start thinking about money, but they might worry about their jobs, whether they will be humiliated by having their weaknesses identified and so on. It is important that people understand exactly why the changes are needed and what (if anything) it means to them.

7. Failing to set out a robust plan

Aircraft need a 'flight plan' to tell them about their flight and organisations need a map to plan the implementation of Lean. Failing to set out a planned journey for your Lean programme from the start is a key way to make it go wrong, waste time and effort as well as end up tackling the wrong issues.

8. Not allocating sufficient resources

There is no magic bullet for Lean and many organisations think that it can be achieved by being an additional task slotted into the diary of busy people. To be successful, Lean requires long-term commitment and regular management involvement.

Having said all of this, the most important thing to remember is that whilst the process of going Lean is hard work, if done properly, it will be beneficial for all stakeholders.

Chapter 7 Self Assessment Questions

• Who is the Improvement Sponsor within your organisation?

• Have previous improvement activities in your organisation addressed the behavioural as well as process change?

• Which of the top 8 problems has your organisation encountered in previous improvement initiatives?

• How much resource can your organisation commit to its Lean programme?

About the Author

Mark Eaton MSc MBA CEng FRSA

Starting his career as a designer in the defence industry, Mark subsequently branched out into manufacturing where he held a number of senior roles in blue chip manufacturing organisations in the defence, aerospace and media industries, working to introduce Lean Concepts in the years before Lean got its current name.

Latterly, Mark moved into consultancy and was involved in a number of high profile regional and national Lean programmes for various public organisations, including the DTi's flagship Transformation Programme for manufacturing in a number of UK regions. For his work, Mark was awarded the Viscount Nuffield Medal in 2004 for his contribution to UK Industry.

In addition to extensive experience of Lean in manufacturing, Mark has also led significant transformation within the Armed Forces and wider public sector before finding a passion for working within the Healthcare Sector where he has worked with a wide range of healthcare organisations and across entire health economies, as well as providing strategic level advice to SHAs and organisations such as the NPSA.

Mark is a Chartered Engineer and has over 50 published articles on topics related to innovation, Lean and sustainable improvement. Mark has also helped write a number of public policy documents, including both regional Innovation and Manufacturing Strategies, and he continues to provide advice and support to a variety of institutes and public bodies.

Appendix 1

Lean Dictionary

2P: (aka Rapid Planning Events) Standing for Process Planning, 2P is the process of preparing an area or organisation for improvement and is often used to 'de-risk' a process prior to implementation. Related to 3P (various definitions but most commonly Production Process Planning) that is used to develop new products, processes and services.

5 Principles: The 5 Principles of Lean as first defined by 'Womack & Jones' in their book Lean Thinking and standing for 'Value, Value Stream, Flow, Pull, Perfection'.

5 Second Rule: A key concept of the 'Visual Workplace' in that problems/issues/status should be visible to an informed person in less than 5 seconds.

5 Why's: (aka Root Cause Analysis) A process of asking 'Why?' five times to uncover the potential root cause of problems that have been encountered.

7 Wastes: (aka WORMPIT) The seven main 'Wastes' (or Non-Value Adding activity), plus the waste of 'Talent', namely, Waiting, Over-Processing, Rework (Correction), Motion

(& Transport), Processing Waste, Inventory and Talent.

Andon: A visual system (often a light) that provides a signal to managers/supervisors when abnormalities occur within processes.

Autonomation: (also called Jidoka) Sometimes referred to as 'automation with a human touch', this is the process of automatically stopping processes rather than allowing large numbers of problems or errors to build up.

Autonomous Maintenance: A concept from TPM (Total Productive Maintenance) where the 'operator' takes responsibility for basic maintenance and servicing of the equipment they use to reduce 'downtime'.

Batch Processing: The process of undertaking work (such as processing patients or producing products) in 'batches' and is the antithesis of 'One Piece Flow'.

Cells: An arranged collection of people, equipment, machines, materials and methods such that activities occur in sequence with minimum waste and so that the area can achieve 'Continuous Flow'

Chaku-Chaku: (aka Load-Load) Used in One Piece Flow systems (ideally where machines automatically unload parts) so that a worker can rapidly move a part through a process from one machine to the next without having to unload parts.

Continuous Flow: (aka One Piece Flow) A process where items are processed and moved one 'piece' at a time, ideally in a process where one item is completed just before the next part of the process requires it.

Cycle Time: (aka Lead Time) The total elapsed time from the start to the end of a 'process' (i.e. Clock Start to Clock Stop), including the sum of all Value Adding and Non-Value Adding time.

Demand: The frequency with which services/products need to be produced based on 'Customer Demand'.

FIFO: Standing for 'First In, First Out', this is the process of dealing with activities strictly in the sequence that they are presented at the 'front door'.

Flow: The process of arranging activities such that bottlenecks, delays between stages and other losses are minimised and the process is capable of 'Continuous Flow'.

Gemba: A Japanese term meaning 'the actual place' where value is added (such as a Clinic/

Theatre or Shop-Floor).

Hand-Off Chart: A diagrammatic representation of a process showing how information/products/ patients, etc. are 'handed off' from one person to another.

Heijunka: The process of levelling demand in variation and mix of product/activity over a fixed time period.

Jishuken: A Japanese word used to describe a 'hands-on knowledge workshop.'

Jidoka: (see Autonomation).

Kaikaku: (another name for Rapid Improvement Events) A process of 'radical improvements', also called such things as 'Step Change' and 'Breakthrough'.

Kaizen: (also commonly thought of a Continuous Improvement) Kaizen comes from the Japanese for 'to improve for the better' in incremental steps.

Kaizen Event: (aka Rapid Improvement Event) See Kaikaku.

Kanban: (aka Pull) Kanban means 'signal' and Kanban is used to trigger demand for an activity, product or service.

Kanban Post: A storage container for Kanban cards that are 'signalling' the need for a product/ service to be delivered.

Lead Time: See Cycle Time

Leader Standard   The activities undertaken by supervisors
Work: and/or managers to sustain and maintain
                        the benefits achieved through Rapid
                        Improvement Events, including Control
                        Boards, MBWA and Audits
                        (including a 5S Audit)

Lean: A business improvement strategy based
                        on the Toyota Production System and
                        designed to eliminate 'waste' and improve
                        effectiveness in processes.

Machine/Manual   The actual time spent on a Machine
Cycle Time: (Machine Cycle Time) or the total amount
                        of work undertaken (Manual Cycle Time)
                        within a process.

MBWA: Standing for 'Management By Walking
                        About' and being the process of managers
                        showing interest in processes and finding
                        solutions by 'going to Gemba' and
                        interacting with staff and customers.

Mistake Proofing: See Poka-Yoke.

Muda: (aka Waste) The Japanese word for 'Non-
                        Value Adding Activity'.

Mura: A Japanese word meaning variation or
                        fluctuation.

Muri: A Japanese work used to mean

'overburdening' or 'unreasonableness'.

Nemawashi: From a Japanese expression meaning to 'prepare the ground for planting', this is used to describe the practice of engaging people and gaining 'buy in' for the change process.

Non-Value-Adding Activity (NVA): (aka Waste and Muda) An activity that uses up time, cost, resources or space but does not add value to the product/ activity itself. Normally identified as things that the customer does not 'value' and would not pay for (if they had to).

One Piece Flow: See Continuous Flow.

Overall Equipment Effectiveness (OEE): A measure used within TPM (Total Productive Maintenance) to describe how effectively equipment (or a Process) is being used and is calculated by multiplying the % availability rate by the % performance rate by the % quality rate.

Overproduction (Over-Processing): The worst form of 'waste' or Non-Value Adding activity is to produce more things than are needed or do more work than is required.

Pacemaker: A part of a process that is a bottleneck and needs to be scheduled to ensure the smooth flow of the rest of the process.

Plan, Do, Study, Act (PDSA): A modified form of PDCA (Plan, Do, Check, Act) first defined by Deming in the 1950s.

PDSA is the form used in healthcare.

Pitch: The amount of time required by an area to go through one cycle of work (and produce one 'container' of products or outputs) and calculated by multiplying Takt Time by the quantity of activity done in each 'pack'.

Poka-Yoke: (aka Mistake Proofing) The process of designing out (or mitigating) the risk of problems arising in a process.

Pull: See Kanban, but also used as a term to mean 'to draw materials/equipment/people to me' in opposition to a 'Push System' (see below).

Push: The production of goods, or 'push' of activity, irrespective of the ability of the downstream process to 'consume' the product or activity.

Rapid Improvement Event (RIE): See Kaikaku.

Rapid Planning Event (RPE): See 2P

Runner, Repeater, Stranger: Runners are activities undertaken 'regularly' (normally every day), Repeaters are common activities that occur less frequently than Runners (say weekly to monthly) and Strangers are activities that come up rarely. In addition, sometimes the term 'Alien' is added to Runner, Repeater, Stranger, to indicate completely unexpected activities.

Safety Stock: Material held to compensate for variations in the process and in supply.

Sensei: Meaning 'Teacher' in Japanese and normally applied to people with a deep understanding of Lean.

Set-Up Time: The amount of time required to 'changeover' a process and measured from the end of the last activity of type 'A' until the first good activity undertaken of type 'B'.

Single Minute Exchange of Die (SMED): A process designed to reduce set-up or changeover times and therefore the creation of a 'Continuous Flow' system.

String Diagram: (aka Spaghetti Diagram) A chart tracing a line showing the path taken by a physical item (such as mobile X-ray) or person during an activity or process.

Standard Work: The process of formerly defining the work method, the tools, staff, quality, inventory and sequence of activities undertaken in a process.

Supermarket: A stack of parts (or people) used to supply an area or process.

Takt Time: Meaning 'beat rate', Takt Time is the rate of demand by customers for activity or products and is calculated by dividing Available Time (i.e. the hours worked per day or shift) by the rate of Customer Orders or Demand.

Total Productive Maintenance (TPM): A process for improving efficiency by eliminating the down time in a process through activities such as 'Autonomous Maintenance'.

Toyota Production System (TPS): The production system developed by the Toyota Motor Company that focuses on the elimination of waste throughout the value stream.

Value Adding Activity: Any activity that 'transforms' the product (or patient) in some way and that is something that the 'customer' is willing to pay for (if they had to).

Value Stream Map (VSM): A detailed process map showing all the steps involved in a process from 'end-to-end' (E2E).

Visual Workplace: (aka Visualisation) The design of a work area such that the status and problems can be identified immediately and that follow the '5 Second Rule'

Voice of the Customer (VotC): The concept of listening to what a customer group really wants from your products and services and then designing your processes to deliver what customers see as 'value adding'.

Waste: See Non-Value Adding Activity.

Work-in-Process (WIP): Work that has started 'production' but has not yet completed.

WORMPIT: See 7 Wastes.

Appendix 2: 5S Audit Form

Area	Check Question	0	1	2	3	4	5
Sort Score____	Are there unneeded items in the area?						
	Is there any equipment or other materials that are being held but not used?						
	Is there any unused paperwork or equipment in the area?						
	Is it obvious which items are current and in use?						
Set Score____	Is it obvious what is supposed to happen in the area?						
	Are signs for storage places for documents and equipment in place and correct?						
	Are all shelved and stored items labelled and located correctly?						
	Are the purposes of different areas clearly marked and are they correct?						
Shine Score____	Are the work areas and floors tidy and free of clutter?						
	Are items returned to their 'home' locations at the end of every working day or shift?						
	Are the required equipment and materials available?						
	Do staff know where things should be located and are they returning them there?						

Appendix 2: 5S Audit Form

Standardise	Does everyone understand the purpose of their 5S activities?					
	Do staff know where things should be located and are they returning them there?					
	Is there a clear improvement plan for each area?					
Score_____	Are there clear instructions visible for how to operate the area's 5S process?					
Sustain	Do employees implement the 5S process consistently?					
	Is there a regular audit schedule to monitor 5S performance?					
	Does the area leader take an active interest in 5S and the actions arising?					
Score_____	Do employees & managers take action to correct low scores on the 5S Audit?					
Total Score (Maximum Score 100)						

Guide to Scoring the Audit

5 = Exceptional – no room for improvement
4 = Very good / could be used as best practice example
3 = Good / requirements exceeded in some areas
2 = Acceptable / requirements met
1 = More effort required to make improvements
0 = No improvement made or no evidence available

Appendix 3

Failure Modes & Effects Analysis (FMEA) Form

Risk Priority Number = Severity x Occurrence x Detection

Items/Process:	Notes/References:	Prepared by:
FMEA Date	Name:	Name:
Sheet Number of	Name:	

Risk Number	Potential Failure Mode	Potential Effects of Failure	Severity (1–10)	Potential Causes of Failure	Occurrence (1–10)	Current Controls	Detection (1–10)	Risk Priority Number	Notes

Appendix 4

Example Scoping Meeting Agenda

A **Scoping Meeting** lasts 3-4 hours and the outcome is an agreed plan (or Scoping Paper) that details what you are attempting to achieve through your programme for improvement. The plan is created by a group which ideally includes representatives from all areas affected, and the resulting document should be widely communicated. Experience says that an effective Scoping Paper can double the probability that your programme will achieve the outcomes you are looking for. This short document sets out how to run a **Scoping Meeting**.

PRIOR TO THE SCOPING MEETING	COMPLETE ✓
Agree Attendee list with a minimum of: • Project Sponsor (Director) • Process Owners (Area Managers affected) • Change Agents (any internal improvement staff who will support the project)	
Gather Background Data	
Prepare an 'Opening Statement' for the Scoping Meeting, which normally consists of: • What is the topic/issue or area that needs improvement? • Why is it important to us (including any background information)? • What would we like to change and by when would we like it changed?	

SCOPING MEETING AGENDA	
AGENDA ITEM	**DESCRIPTION**
• Opening Statement	Review opening statement created prior to the event

Example Scoping Meeting Agenda (cont.)

• Open Discussion	Deal with any questions or clarification requirements
• Develop Compelling Need	Create an inspiring statement that details why this project must happen
• Fix Measures of Success	Outline 3–5 critical measures of success for the programme
• Identify 'Scenarios'	Outline scenarios which fully 'test' the pathways to be improved
• Outline who is 'In Scope'	Detail which areas (and individuals) are going to be involved FT/PT
• Outline the 'Fixed Points'	Outline the 'boundaries', risks and anything which cannot be changed
• Identify 'Key Roles'	Identify the 'Improvement Sponsor' & 'Change Agents'
• Set out your 'Activity Plan'	Set out the plan for activities associated with the project
• Fix your Communications	Identify how the 'Scoping Paper' will be communicated

AFTER THE SCOPING MEETING	COMPLETE ✓
Complete the 'Scoping Paper' and add in any missing detail	
Communicate the 'Scoping Paper'	
Plan for the 'Next Steps' in the Programme	

Appendix 5

Guide to running a Value Stream Mapping Event

This guide is provided to Change Agents who are required to plan and lead Value Stream Mapping Events (VSE). This document should be viewed as an 'aide memoire', and the experience of the Change Agent should be used to fill in the gaps as no document can ever replace true experience.

What is a Value Stream Mapping Event (VSE)?

Variously called such things as Value Stream Analysis or Pathway Redesign, Value Stream Mapping Events (VSE) are used to transform end-to-end pathways and processes such as Orthopaedics, the Commissioning Cycle or Emergency Care.

A VSE is a three-stage process that begins by looking at how the service/area is currently run (called 'Current State'), and then goes through a two-stage redesign process to create a realistic 'Future State' and a corresponding implementation plan.

You should aim to plan your VSEs around a 9-Week Cycle, although this sometimes has to be extended in healthcare and other public sector environments to allow time for people to be released from commitments to enable them to participate in events.

Value Stream Mapping Events FAQs

This section tackles some of the Frequently Asked Questions (FAQs) that people often ask about Value Stream Mapping Events.

How many VSEs to run per year?

In terms of how many to run, this is a subjective matter for the organisation concerned. A VSE will typically identify between 10 and 30 implementation activities. Some of these will be simple actions but it is reasonable to suggest that a typical pathway will identify 3–9 Rapid Improvement Events. Therefore, undertaking 8 VSEs in a year will generate some 48 Rapid Improvement Events (see below for a guide to running Rapid Improvement Events). Therefore, the organisation needs to decide how much 'downstream' activity it wants to commit itself to.

How many people per event?

Well, again this will vary depending on the needs of the event and the scope. However, 8–10 is a common team size, although they have run successfully with 3–4 (for small events) or up to 30 for a larger event, but above around 15 people per pathway the team dynamics become more difficult to manage.

How long do they last?

VSEs can last from three days to around five days. The variation in duration comes from the fact that pathways vary in complexity and the depth in which you need to go to obtain an effective outcome.

What are the outcomes?

The outcome of a VSE is normally an agreed 'Future State' and an implementation plan. An implementation plan can be created on 'brown paper' or on a software package such as Visio or Leanpad for Healthcare.

The Value Stream Mapping Event (VSE)

We have had to base this short document on a 5-day VSE, but we recognise that not all events need to be five days long.

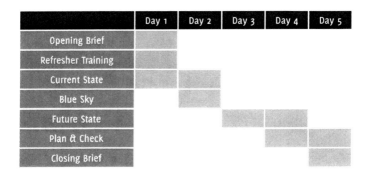

	Day 1	Day 2	Day 3	Day 4	Day 5
Opening Brief					
Refresher Training					
Current State					
Blue Sky					
Future State					
Plan & Check					
Closing Brief					

Fitting the Value Stream Mapping Event into its 9-Week Cycle

The next diagram shows how the VSE Event Week (shown as VSE below) fits into a full nine weeks of activity. The diagram shows the three phases of a VSE: prepare for the VSE, the event and prepare for implementation.

As mentioned above, the period of preparation might need to be extended to allow longer for people to be released, which is particularly the case in healthcare and in local government.

Week	1	2	3	4	5	6	7	8	9
Prepare for the VSE									
The VSE									
Prepare for Implementation									

Fitting Value Stream Mapping Events into a larger programme

The last diagram shows how a VSE might fit into an overall programme of implementation. In this example, there is a requirement for six RIEs and the programme is spread over eight months.

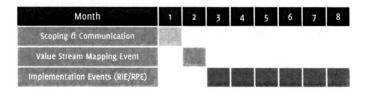

The three main approaches for implementation used by organisations to implement Lean are detailed below, although it is important to state that other approaches to implementing improvement might also be required:

- ⊙ Rapid Improvement Event – an event focused on implementing one or more elements or actions that come from the Value Stream Mapping Event.

- ⊙ Rapid Planning Event – also called a 2P/3P event, this event is used to 'de-risk' critical processes prior to implementation.

- ⊙ Focused Improvement Team – a team brought together to focus on tackling a specific issue or implementing a specific change where a Rapid Improvement Event is not feasible (perhaps due to time/resource constraints or for lower priority projects).

Value Stream Mapping Events (9-Week Plan)

The following is an idealised approach to VSE based on a 9-Week Cycle. There is a certain amount of flexibility required in how events are planned and run and therefore this checklist should only be used as a guide by experienced Change Agents. Obviously, we have already mentioned that the timescales in the Prepare Phase may need to be adjusted to provide additional time for personnel to be released from their work commitments to participate.

PREPARE PHASE

WEEK 1	COMPLETE
Agree who will Sponsor (Champion) the programme of improvement	
Scope the Value Stream Mapping Event (VSE)	
Set the date of the VSE and identify those who will be involved	
Communicate the dates/timing of the event	
WEEK 2	**COMPLETE**
Walk the process to be focused on	
Gather the 'Top 10 Hurts' from the wider team affected by the processes	
Gather key data (Demand Rate, Takt Time, MCT, Incidents, Costs, Performance, etc.)	
Prioritise the issues to be tackled and identify how they can be grouped together	
Identify how the participants will be deployed and a 'Team Leader' for the event	
WEEK 3	**COMPLETE**
Brief the entire team affected by the process (not just those participating)	
Prepare an event kit (post-its, brown paper, tape, paint, etc. as appropriate)	
Undertake Lean awareness training for the Event Team as a minimum	
WEEK 4	**COMPLETE**
Ensure all participants are still ok to attend for the whole event	
Confirm the schedule, event objectives and venue again	
Brief the Event Sponsor on their 'Opening Brief'	
Publicise the event's Closing Brief date/time	
Confirm all data is available and ensure there are no outstanding Week 1–4 activities	

THE VALUE STREAM MAPPING EVENT

In the event phase, we have assumed the VSE is planned to run over five days. Obviously a different, but broadly similar approach, will be required for shorter events.

DAY 1	COMPLETE
Opening Brief given by the Event Sponsor (or another senior representative)	
Undertake a short refresher training session	
Review the available data and information about the event	
Analyse the current state using tools such as Process Analysis, String Diagrams, etc.	
Daily Closing Brief given by the event team to the wider area team and interested others	

DAY 2	COMPLETE
Review the Current State from Day 1 & Finalise	
Create a summary of the key facts about the process (duration, number of steps etc)	
Discuss the creation of an Ideal (or Blue Sky) State and introduce Lean symbols	
Undertake a Blue Sky review and identify ideas for improvement	
Daily Closing Brief (as Day 1)	

DAY 3	COMPLETE
Review Day 1 & 2	
Identify any questions that need to be answered and any data that needs to be collected	
Start to create a 'Future State'	
Daily Closing Brief (as Day 1)	

DAY 4	COMPLETE
Review Day 1,2 & 3	
Identify any questions that need to be answered and any data that needs to be collected	
Finalise 'Future State' & Start to create an Implementation Plan	
Daily Closing Brief (as Day 1)	

EMBEDDING PHASE

DAY 5	DAY
Finalise implementation plan	
Review any actions still 'To Do'	
Prepare for the 'Closing Brief' with the team	
Undertake a dry run for the 'Closing Brief'	
Undertake Closing Brief	
WEEK 6	**COMPLETE**
Communicate the Future State & seek feedback	
Plan for implementation (including first Rapid Improvement Events and other events)	
Establish each implementation activity has an owner and a project plan	
WEEK 7	**COMPLETE**
Revise the Future State based on any feedback	
Continue to plan for implementation	
Review 'To Do' list from the event and close off remaining actions	
WEEK 8	**COMPLET**
Revise the Future State based on any feedback	
Continue to plan for implementation	
Review 'To Do' list from the event and do a final sign-off	
WEEK 9	**COMPLETE**
Aim for first implementation events to commence this week	
Continue to review/update Future State as required	

Value Stream Mapping Event Truisms

The following are some key pointers about Value Stream Mapping Events that should help Change Agents to deal with some of the issues they may encounter.

Badly Prepared Events – If the event is badly prepared or badly supported, don't run it else you will end up the loser!

Celebrate Success, but Accept Occasional Failure – Not all events will be successful, although those that are better prepared are generally less likely to fail. You will need to accept occasional failure (as in events that do not deliver what is required) as part of the journey to improvement, and so does your boss!

Big Bang or Drip Drip! – Not all the benefits of the event will be identified during the VSE itself, and that means that having a process of Continuous Improvement will be needed for you to get the best results!

Experience Tells – Basic experience of running VSEs can be gained through running two or three, but real experience comes after you have got at least 10 events under your belt as by that time you will have seen nearly every type of activity/issue that can arise, but only if they are well run and varied events – 10 similar events will not give you the breadth of experience!

Appendix 6

Guide to running a Rapid Improvement Event

This guide is provided to Change Agents who are required to plan and lead events. This document should be viewed as an 'aide memoire' and the experience of the Change Agent should be used to fill in the gaps as no document can ever replace true experience.

What is a Rapid Improvement Event (RIE)?

Variously called such things as Kaizen Events, Kaizen Blitzes, Lean Weeks, Improvement Workshops, etc., a Rapid Improvement Event (RIE) is a process of systematically implementing changes to the way products and services are delivered. The outcomes of an RIE are improved processes.

The RIE itself is broken into three phases: before, during and after. You should aim to plan your RIEs around a 9-Week Cycle, although this sometimes has to be extended in healthcare and other public sector environments to allow time for people to be released from commitments to enable them to participate in events.

Rapid Improvement Events FAQs

This section tackles some of the Frequently Asked Questions (FAQs) that people often ask about Rapid Improvement Events (RIEs).

How many RIEs to run per year?

In terms of how many to run, this is a subjective matter for the organisation concerned. If the organisation has 2,000 employees and wants to engage all of them in RIEs within a reasonable period (under three years perhaps) then, assuming each RIE normally has a team of around 8–10, this will mean approximately 200 events over three years, meaning around 70 per year. Of course, in the first year the organisation will normally go slower than 70 and by Year 3 you would expect that many events will be self-initiated. This short document does not cover the cultural and organisational changes and structures that are required to achieve this pace of change.

As a rule of thumb for organisations of over 500 employees, to calculate the number of RIEs required during Year 1 of a programme take the number of people involved and divide this number by 20–25, in Year 2 divide the number by 15–20 and in Year 3 by 10–15. The resulting number is the quantity of Rapid Improvement Events you need to run if you want to engage all of your team. Obviously, if you are only working with a percentage of your organisation you will need to run fewer RIEs.

How many people per event?

Well, again this will vary depending on the needs of the event and the scope. However, 8–10 is a common team size, although they have run successfully with 3–4 (for small events) or up to 30 for a larger event. Above this size it is normal to sub-divide the team to focus on different events.

How long do they last?

RIEs can last from less than one day up to five days. The duration of the event needs to match the size of the event and sometimes organisations will group together a number of smaller events into one larger event.

What are the outcomes?

The term Rapid Improvement Events can be confusing, especially as they are used in different ways by different people and organisations. Fundamentally though, Rapid Improvement Events are a process used to implement Lean Changes (such as Visual Management, Standard Work, Mistake Proofing, Flow, etc.) and therefore any event that results in a plan (such as a Future State) is not normally an RIE.

The Rapid Improvement Event Week

We have had to base this short document on a 5-day Rapid Improvement Event, but we recognise that not all events need to be five days long. However, putting the RIE in context, the first figure below shows the broad breakdown of activity during a single 'Event Week':

	Day 1	Day 2	Day 3	Day 4	Day 5
Opening Brief	▨				
Refresher Training	▨				
Review Current State	▨				
Design & Test Options		▨	▨		
Implement Solutions			▨	▨	
Prepare for the Embed Stage				▨	▨
Closing Brief					▨

Fitting the Rapid Improvement Event into its 9-Week Cycle

The next diagram shows how the RIE Event Week (shown as RIE below) fits into a full nine weeks of activity. The diagram shows the three phases of a RIE: prepare for the event, the event itself and embed/improve the changes.

As mentioned above, the period of preparation might need to be extended to allow longer for people to be released, which is particularly the case in healthcare and the wider public sector.

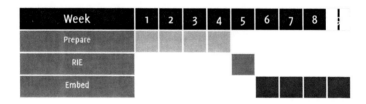

Fitting Rapid Improvement Events into a larger programme

The last diagram below shows how individual RIEs fit into an overall programme of redesign (say in an end-to-end clinical pathway in healthcare) where there is a requirement for more than a single Rapid Improvement Event. In this example, there is a requirement for five RIEs and the programme is spread over seven months.

Month	1	2	3	4	5	6	
Scoping & Communication							
Redesign End-to-End Pathway							
Rapid Improvement Events			RIE 1	RIE 2	RIE 3	RIE 4	RIE 5

The two main approaches used by most organisations to implement changes other than Rapid Improvement Events are detailed below, but it is important to state that other approaches to implementing improvement might also be required.

- **Rapid Planning Event** – also called a 2P/3P event, this event is used to 'de-risk' critical processes prior to implementation.

- **Focused Improvement Team** – a team brought together to focus on tackling a specific issue or implementing a specific change where a Rapid Improvement Event is not feasible (perhaps due to time/resource constraints or for lower priority projects).

Rapid Improvement Events (9-Week Plan)

The following is an idealised approach to Rapid Improvement Events based on a 9-Week Cycle. There is a certain amount of flexibility required in how events are planned and run and therefore this checklist should only be used as a guide by experienced Change Agents. Obviously, we have already mentioned that the timescales in the Prepare Phase may need to be adjusted to provide additional time for personnel to be released from their work commitments to participate.

PREPARE PHASE

WEEK 1	COMPLETE
Agree who will Sponsor (i.e. champion) the event and the venue	
Agree the Event Objectives and the area to be focused on (and boundaries of the event)	
Identify the participants for the event and any support team (IT, procurement etc.)	
Communicate the dates/timing of the event	
Plan for how any disruption to the area being focused on can be minimised and/or managed	
WEEK 2	**COMPLETE**
Walk the process to be focused on	
Gather the 'Top 10 Hurts' from the wider team affected by the processes	
Gather key data (Demand Rate, Takt Time, MCT, Incidents, Costs, Performance, etc.)	
Prioritise the issues to be tackled and identify how they can be grouped together	
Identify how the participants will be deployed and a 'Team Leader' for the event	
WEEK 3	**COMPLETE**
Complete 5S Audit	
Complete Event Summary Form detailing the specific objectives of the event	
Brief the entire team affected by the process (not just those participating)	
Prepare an event kit (post-its, brown paper, tape, paint, etc. as appropriate)	
Undertake Lean awareness training for the Event Team as a minimum	
WEEK 4	**COMPLETE**
Ensure all participants are still ok to attend for the whole event	
Confirm the schedule, event objectives and venue again	
Brief the Event Sponsor on their 'Opening Brief'	
Publicise the event's Closing Brief date/time	
Confirm all data is available and ensure there are no outstanding Week 1-4 activities	

THE RAPID IMPROVEMENT EVENT WEEK

In the Event Phase, we have assumed the Rapid Improvement Event is planned to run over five days. Obviously a different, but broadly similar approach, will be required for shorter events. Also, this profile is used for operationally focused processes (i.e. front-line service delivery processes) and a different approach will be used for more strategic or administrative processes.

DAY 1	COMPLETE
Opening Brief given by the Event Sponsor (or another senior representative)	
Review the available data and information about the event	
Gather real facts about the process (string diagrams, process maps, paper layouts, etc.)	
Identify opportunities for improvement	
Daily Closing Brief given by the event team to the wider area team and interested others	

DAY 2	COMPLETE
Review Day 1	
Design solutions (Design 5, Rational Decision Making, etc.)	
Test selected solution (Simulation, Cardboard Engineering)	
Prepare for implementation	
Daily Closing Brief (as Day 1)	

DAY 3	COMPLETE
Finalise move of equipment and ensure process 'Flows'	
Start to implement Visual Management	
Start to create Standard Work	
Establish monitoring system for new process	
Daily Closing Brief (as Day 1)	

DAY 4	COMPLETE
Finalise Visual Management	
Finalise Standard Work	
Observe/time new process and identify further improvements (20+ Improvements)	
Prepare list of outstanding issues	
Daily Closing Brief (as Day 1 if appropriate)	

DAY 5	COMPLETE
Finalise all event activities including plan for the embedding phase (Weeks 6–9)	
Calculate and quantify the benefits of the event and undertake a 5S+1 Audit	
Prepare a 'Follow Up' plan of things to do	
Undertake a dry run for the 'Closing Brief'	
Undertake Event Closing Brief (given by team)	

EMBEDDING PHASE

WEEK 6	COMPLET
Review the 'Follow Up' list and ensure all tasks have an owner	
Review the revised processes and walk through the new process	
Review the Standard Work & Visual Management implemented to ensure it is working	
Undertake Daily 5S Audit & identify opportunities for further improvement	
Undertake Continuous Improvement Review	

WEEK 7	COMPLET
Review the 'Follow Up' list and ensure all tasks are progressing toward completion	
Bring the event team together to discuss the progress to date	
Review the Standard Work & Visual Management implemented to ensure it is still working	
Undertake 5S Audit at least three times during the week	
Undertake Continuous Improvement Review	

WEEK 8	COMPLET
Review the 'Follow Up' list and ensure all tasks are progressing toward completion	
Get sign-off from the Event Sponsor on the projected/realised quantified event benefits	
Review the Standard Work & Visual Management implemented	
Undertake 5S Audit at least two times during the week	
Undertake Continuous Improvement Review	

WEEK 9	COMPLET
Review the 'Follow Up' list and ensure all tasks are closed off or planned for close off	
Create an Event Case Study and get it signed off by the Event Sponsor	
Help the Event Sponsor to plan the next phase of improvement in the area	
Undertake final 5S Audit	
Undertake Close Out Meeting and hand over control to the Event Sponsor	

Appendix 7

A Lean Parable for Practitioners everywhere

Once upon a time there lived a man named Clarence who had a pet frog named Eric. Clarence lived a modestly comfortable existence on what he earned working at the local supermarket, but he always dreamed of being rich.

"Eric!" Clarence exclaimed one day, "We're going to be rich! I'm going to teach you how to fly!" Eric, of course, was terrified at the prospect. "I can't fly, you idiot! I'm a frog, not a canary!"

Clarence, disappointed at the initial reaction, told Eric "That negative attitude of yours could be a real problem. I'm sending you on a training course." So Eric went on a three-day training course and learned all about problem solving, time management, and effective communication, etc., but nothing about flying.

After the course was over, Clarence could barely control his excitement. He explained that the block of flats in which they lived had 15 floors, and each day Eric would jump out of a window starting with the first floor, eventually getting to the top floor. After each jump, Eric would analyse how well he flew, focus on the most effective flying techniques, and implement the improved process for the next flight. By the time they reached the top floor, Eric would surely be able to fly.

Eric pleaded for his life, but it fell on deaf ears. He just doesn't understand how important this is, thought Clarence, but I won't let 'naysayers' get in the way. With that, Clarence opened the window and threw Eric out. He landed with a thud.

Next day, poised for his second flying lesson, Eric again begged not to be thrown out of the window. With that Clarence opened his pocket guide to Managing More Effectively and showed Eric the part about how one must always expect resistance when implementing new programmes. And with that, he threw him out of the window. (THUD)

On the third day (at the third floor window), Eric tried a different ploy: stalling. He asked for a delay in the project until better weather would make flying conditions more favourable. But Clarence was ready for him. He produced a project timeline and pointed to the third milestone and asked "You don't want to miss the deadline, do you?"

From his training Eric knew that not jumping today would mean that he would have to jump TWICE tomorrow and with a sigh like a gentle wind he quietly said "OK. Let's go." (THUD)

Now this is not to say that Eric wasn't trying his best. On the fourth day he flapped his feet madly in a vain attempt to fly. THUD. On the fifth day he tied a small red cape around his neck and tried to think like Superman. But try as he may, he couldn't fly.

By the sixth day, Eric, accepting his fate, no longer begged for mercy. He looked pointedly at Clarence and said "You know you're killing me, don't you?"

Clarence pointed out that Eric's performance so far had been less than exemplary, failing to meet any of the milestone goals he had set for him.

With that, Eric said quietly "Shut up and open the window." And he leaped out, taking careful aim on the large jagged rock by the corner of the building.

So Eric went to the great lily pad in the sky.

Clarence was extremely upset, as his project had failed to meet a single goal that he set out to accomplish.

Eric had not only failed to fly, he didn't even learn to steer his flight as he fell like a sack of cement ... nor did he improve when Clarence told him to fall smarter, not harder.

The only thing left for Clarence to do was to analyse the process and try to determine where it had gone wrong.

After much thought, Clarence smiled and said "Next time ... I'm getting a smarter frog!"

Lesson of this parable

Not all roadblocks and concerns that people raise during Lean Events are diversionary – some of them genuinely need to be addressed!

Appendix 8

Skills plan for Lean People

The following is a summary of the expected experience, skills, behaviours and competences that are required for the four main groups of people who will be involved in Lean programmes.

	Aware	Participant (Basic)	Participant (Advanced)	Practitioner	Leader
Experience	0-1 Lean Events	0-5 Lean Events	5-20 Lean Events	20-40 Lean Events	40+ Lean Events
Skills	• Basic Lean Awareness • Lean Principles	As Previous + • Rapid Improvement Events • Rapid Planning Events	As Previous + • Value Stream Mapping Events • Risk Management Tools • Basic Facilitation Skills	As Previous + • Facilitation Skills • Change Management • Project Management Skills	As Previous + • Train the Trainer • Mentoring Skills
Behaviours & Competences	Open to participating in Lean Events	Ability to participate and support Lean Events and to help change the mindset of others	Able to initiate simple events, deal with queries and support continuous improvement	Ability to initiate and lead complex events and inspire people to get involved	Ability to manage multiple work-streams, motivate teams and deal with the most complex of events

Appendix 9

Lean By The Dozen Article

This article was first published by the Institute of Operations
Management in their journal control and has been adapted for
inclusion in *Lean for Practitioners*.

Abstract

Even with the current economic conditions, Lean is alive and
well across a range of sectors. This article provides an overview
of some of the key historical events that have helped shape
Lean today as well as a review of the state of Lean in the UK
today in the public, service and manufacturing sectors. Based
on discussions with Lean consultancies, organisations and desk
research, we will show that whilst the downturn in the economy
is also driving a downturn in the investment in Lean in some
areas, there is a real benefit in adopting Lean to enable your
organisation to survive in difficult times as well as prepare for
the future, whichever way it goes.

Introduction to Lean by the Dozen

Most of the goals and principles of Lean are common sense.
Benjamin Franklin in his *Poor Richard's Almanac* (published
from 1732 to 1758) says of wasted time, "He that idly loses
five shilling's worth of time, loses five shillings and might as
prudently throw five shillings into the river." Franklin further
added that avoiding unnecessary costs could be as (or more)
profitable as increasing sales, stating "A penny saved is two
pence clear."

In this article we will take a look back at the history and some of the key milestones that have led to the development of Lean as it stands today and then provide a look at the state of Lean today in the public and private sector.

We will end with a short discussion about the possible future for Lean in the UK given where the economy may go in the next two years.

The Origins of Lean

Because Lean contains many elements that are intuitive (such as the desire to maximise productivity and ensure that waste is minimised) the history of Lean can be difficult to trace as much of what went before 1996 when the term 'Lean' was coined would have appeared as 'good practice' at the time and not necessarily have been seen as part of the development of a structured approach to transformation. Like much in the history of human development, it is the bringing together of many factors that has led to the development of Lean including the availability of tested methods, expertise to turn those methods into actions and the need for the methods (in the form of improved efficiency) that has driven its development.

In the Table below, I have provided a summary Lean timeline containing just a few of the many milestones that have led the way to today's Lean movement. In the process of selecting items to include, I have had to miss out many more than I have put in including the importance of the US supermarket chain Piggly Wiggly in helping Toyota develop the concepts of the Toyota Production System, and the work of the 18th Century economist Adam Smith in helping shape an economic environment in which businesses can have the freedom (and funds) to invest in Lean, but the box contains some of the most frequently cited examples of key Lean milestones.

The Lean Timeline

- From 1473 – The Venice Arsenal develop a 'continuous flow' process based on mass produced and standardised items that ultimately enables them to produce an entire ship in around one day.

- 1776 – Lieutenant General Jean-Baptist de Gribeauval becomes Inspector of Artillery in France and starts to introduce reforms to reduce the diversity of artillery in use and replacing it with a more standardised range of weapons that also used a form of interchangeable parts and manufacture.

- 1799 Eli Whitney – Inventor of the Cotton Gin takes on the contract to produce 10,000 muskets for the US Army at a low cost of $13.40 each. To enable him to do this he had perfected the process of designing interchangeable parts between the muskets which enabled the process to be divided up and standardised.

- 1894–1912 – Frederick W Taylor publishes a series of articles on improving efficiency, with his key work *Principles of Scientific Management* being published in 1911with details of how to eliminate many of the inefficient practices existing in industry at the time and strongly advocating standardised work and the division of labour to improve efficiency. Collectively this approach is later termed 'Taylorism'.

- 1905–1921 – Frank & Lillian Gilbreth (made famous by the film *Cheaper by the Dozen* in 1950 and indirectly the reason for the name of this article) publish a series of articles and books on improving efficiency through Time & Motion Study, culminating in 1921 with their book *Time & Motion Study As Fundamental Factors in Planning & Control*.

- 1910 – Henry Ford along with Charles E Sorensen create a comprehensive manufacturing strategy and move to the Highland Park Plant, Michigan, which was the world's first automobile plant that used an assembly line, and in 1914 they created the first moving assembly line reducing production times by a further 75%.

- 1924–1939 – Walter Shewhart proposes the statistical control of processes and later his work is adapted by W Edwards Deming to form the 'Plan-Do-Check-Act' cycle and to form the basis of Six Sigma, although many of the concepts are also adopted within a 'Lean' approach to effectiveness.

- 1943 – Taiichi Ohno joins Toyota Motor Corporation and later (1947 onwards) starts the development of what is now known as the 'Toyota Production System' (TPS) incorporating cellular working, waste reduction, reduction of Work in Process (WIP), in-process inspection by workers and many of the other concepts, including (in 2001) the 'respect for people' principle.

- 1983 – Robert Hall publishes *Zero Inventories* which is seen as the first broad description of the Toyota Production System by an American author.

> ○ 1990–1996 –Jim Womack & Dan Jones produce *The machine that changed the world* (1990) and *Lean Thinking* (1996), coining the term Lean and defining the five principles of Lean.

Lean's Place Today

What can be seen by the history of Lean is that it has been a process of adaptation of ideas, incorporation of new thinking and extensive testing and we can only expect this to continue into the future.

In this section we will examine the current state of Lean in three main areas, namely the Public Sector, Service Industries and in its traditional home of Manufacturing. What is clear is that in times of economic uncertainty such as we are currently experiencing, Lean has an even bigger role to play in helping drive out wastes in organisations, but also that these very same organisations are just as likely not to invest in Lean at this time due to the economic pressures, what can be termed a 'no win situation'.

Lean in the Public Sector

Following the publication in 2004 of the Gershon Review (titled 'Releasing resources to the front line') the public sector has been driven by the need both to demonstrate that the services they are buying and providing can be considered 'value for money' and to demonstrate that they are continuing to improve the effectiveness of the services they provide.

Like many manufacturing companies, a large number of public sector organisations have used Lean to deliver short-term improvements in performance to meet their obligations under the 'efficiency agenda', and whilst this has generated some significant gains (such as the reduction in the time taken to process high demand housing adaptations for disabled people in one area from 200 days to 12 days), fewer of them are realising the longer-term organisational benefits that can accrue through the associated cultural change that Lean can bring (most notably in creating an environment that supports continuous improvement) rather than just the short-term cash and resource releasing benefits that can be achieved.

The available evidence suggests that at a local level (such as local councils or individual NHS organisations) there are islands of excellence, but the uptake of Lean is both patchy and in many organisations has been started and then stopped. Some of the factors that seem to underpin this patchwork approach to Lean are the creation of a reliance on an external consultancy that is not transferred to an internal team (and becomes uneconomic to support), a change of management focus (or even a change of management) or simply that Lean was adopted to tackle a short-term strategic issue and was not seen as a long-term concept for organisation, wide change.

However, there are still some very inspiring stories of the use of Lean in the public sector in areas such as HM Revenue & Customs and the NHS, with the latter using Lean to both improve safety and the experience of patients as well as the more traditional use in reducing costs and increasing capacity in places such as theatres and outpatient departments.

With one in five workers in the UK employed in the public sector there is obviously a great scope for Lean to be used to improve efficiency in vital areas such as health and local services, but the reduction in revenues that can be expected due to the current economic conditions will significantly reduce the revenues available to fund the external support that has marked out the growth of Lean in public services, and this will place an increasing need on public sector organisations to 'grow their own' Lean capability.

Lean in the Service Industries

With far more people employed in the service sector than in the traditional industrial sector (with common estimates stating that there are 4-6 service sector jobs for every manufacturing position) there is obviously a large market for Lean, but until recently the 'uptake' of Lean in the service sector has not been as prolific as that seen in the manufacturing sector. Some of this was to do with difficulties in the translation of concepts such as continuous flow and standardised work from an industrial to a service context, but it was also the absence of established success stories that initially prevented service companies from investing in Lean.

Like the history of Lean generally, the history of Lean in the service sector is mixed up with examples of good practice that go back many years, but a good stake in the ground for the start of the efficiency drive in the service sector can be traced to the book *Relevance Lost* by Johnson & Kaplan (1991) which ultimately led to the Lean movement in the accountancy sector.

Attempts to introduce Lean (although it was not called such at the time, being mostly done under the banner of Business Process Re-engineering) into the service sector in the early to mid 1990s tended to fall over because the approaches either did not 'fit' (being too industrial in nature), were too disruptive, for example trying to transform the entire organisation simultaneously, or proponents misused the concepts to dehumanise workplaces.

Over the last 10 years, and with the development of Lean since 1996, there have been an increasing number of case studies of Lean being used in such places as call centres to improve capacity, the energy sector to reduce administrative overheads and the financial services sector (although I am sure the adoption of Lean was not at the centre of the current banking crisis).

There have even been tentative steps taken by various government agencies to promote Lean in the service sector (or Lean Office as it is sometimes also termed to allow it to include the administrative functions of manufacturing companies as well as purely service sector organisations), and there does seem to be a correlation between the availability of case studies, the production of available information and the uptake of Lean in the service sector since 2000, with an increase in any one of these three areas driving an increase in the other two, for example more case studies triggers more published materials and this in turn has an impact on the uptake.

From discussions with organisations actively involved in delivering Lean in the service sector the message is broadly consistent in that those organisations that have seen the benefits of Lean are continuing to invest in reducing costs and improving effectiveness (albeit a number have scaled back the size of their investment), whilst most of those who were toying with Lean prior to the current economic conditions have parked their investment plans for the current time.

The benefits of Lean in the service sector are clear from the many case studies that exist, from reducing the time taken to answer calls to a call centre by 90% through to reducing the costs of processing claims in the insurance sector by 75%, but like the public sector, the focus has to be on developing internal capability rather than creating or continuing the dependence on external consultants, and there are an increasing number of workshops with titles such as 'Lean in the Office', 'Lean Accounting' and 'Lean in Service' that underpin the drive to raise the Lean skills of people in the service sector.

Lean in Manufacturing

Manufacturing is the traditional home of Lean and certainly the one with the greatest number of case studies. In addition, the government has invested heavily in promoting Lean in manufacturing through schemes aimed at raising the number of people with Lean skills (including the promotion of the Lean based Business Improvement Techniques NVQ) and also providing discounted consulting advice to SMEs, but even given the length of time people have had to invest in Lean and get it right there are still a large percentage of manufacturing companies paying lip service to Lean or using it purely as a tactical vehicle for short-term improvements.

The real issues that underpin why manufacturers have had a love/hate relationship with Lean have revolved around their ability to both turn great plans into great benefits and then sustaining the change against forces that want to return to the 'old ways'. Productivity in manufacturing has gone up over the last 15 years although it would be impossible to state how much of this has been due to Lean and how much has been brought about by the changing mix of manufacturing in the UK (away from low cost/low margin producers to higher value add manufacturing), but Lean and similar approaches have certainly played a part in the improvements in many companies.

The application of Lean in manufacturing was initially focused on reducing lead times and the overall amount of work required to produce each item, but latterly has focused on the whole enterprise including the sales and finance functions, stock management, distribution and service. In essence, the focus of Lean for many manufacturing companies is now taking what Professor Michael Porter describes as a 'Value Chain' approach from initial concept through to after-sales service.

The results for those manufacturing companies investing in the cultural as well as the process changes that can be achieved by Lean are seeing a year on year reduction in operating costs, increased flexibility, better customer service and reduced defects, but with the current economic conditions pressing hard on the manufacturing sector, generally many organisations who were previously investing in Lean have either scaled back or stopped their investment completely. The long-term effects of these decisions will be difficult to estimate, but it will certainly introduce an amount of inertia that, when things start to pick up, the organisations will need to overcome again to get their Lean programme back on track.

Lean – Alive & Kicking

What can be seen is that Lean is alive and kicking across most of the UK and even though the current economic conditions have created a 'slow down' in the progress to Lean, it still has a role to play. If the economy continues to be depressed throughout 2009 and into 2010/11 then Lean will be an essential tool for enabling organisations to reduce costs and create flexible and responsive processes.

When the economy starts to recover, Lean can help organisations to achieve 'first mover' advantage as new opportunities appear and it also plays a role in the development of effective new products and services that will meet the growing demand that will signal the start of the recovery.

When back to full strength, Lean has a role to play in creating a culture of continuous improvement that will prepare your organisation not just for the recovery but for any future ups or downs that your market may experience.

Selected Lean Reading

In this list I have introduced some of the many Lean books that now exist to demonstrate the breadth of topics covered.

- The Toyota Way Fieldbook (Liker & Meier) – McGraw-Hill ISBN 978-0-07-144893-2

- Flow in the Office (Venegas) – Productivity Press ISBN 978-1-56327-361-2

- Creating a Lean Culture (Mann) – Productivity Press ISBN 978-1-56327-322-3

- Improving Healthcare Using Toyota Lean Production Methods (Chalice) – ASQ ISBN 978-0-87389-713-6

- Value Stream Management for the Lean Office (Tapping & Shuker) – Productivity Press ISBN 978-1-56327-246-2

- 5S for the Office (Fabrizio & Tapping) – Productivity Press ISBN 978-1-56327-318-6

- The Complete Lean Enterprise (Keyte & Locher) – Productivity Press ISBN 978-1-56327-301-8

Appendix 10

5S for Everyone

This article was first published by the Institute of Operations Management in their journal control and has been adapted for inclusion in *Lean for Practitioners*.

5S for Everyone Introduction

Implementing change doesn't always require 12 months to plan before anything happens. Many organisations spend thousands on poster campaigns, coupled with a detailed and lengthy training programme and the award of certificates before they even get going, and there are examples of organisations where everyone has been obliged to sign a sentence saying "I am committed to change and the implementation of Best Practice".

By the time that everyone has come through this process they have forgotten why it started and probably had any initial enthusiasm drained from them. The art to introducing change is to spend less time planning and more time doing. The use of simple techniques, coupled with good communication about why things need to change and what is happening, along with a modicum of enthusiasm, can have a profound effect at a fraction of the cost.

A personal favourite tool is the application of 5S to a process. It is cheap and effective to implement and the initial (and most dramatic) stages have visible effects within hours of starting the process. Due to the ease of implementing 5S, another key benefit is that it starts to demonstrate that an organisation is 'serious' about change as 'actions speak louder than words'.

In basic terms 5S takes the discussion about the 'C' word ('Change' of course) out of the boardroom and into front-line services.

5S is often quoted as simple housekeeping and indeed the earliest stage has much in common with tidying up and removing rubbish. As many organisations stop after completing the first 'S', it is understandable why people make this comparison. But taking 5S further improves productivity, eliminates waste and creates a smarter, safer environment. Over a sustained period, the added overhead of wasted time and inefficient processes can severely affect both financial performance and safety within the process as well as the experience (and outcomes) for customers (patients).

Originally, 5S came from five Japanese words beginning with S. To aid understanding, equivalent English words beginning with the letter S are used. Different people use different words for the same part of the process (for example many people use the word SHINE, whilst some use SCRUB). Additionally, there are at least two different ways of implementing 5S, but essentially they all have the same final result. The table below shows the original Japanese word and a common English equivalent.

Japanese Word	English Equivalent
Seiri	Sort
Seiton	Set
Seiso	Shine
Seiketsu	Standardise
Shitsuke	Sustain

A simple explanation of each technique is as follows. The first three 'S's' are about 'doing' the change, whilst the last two are about the systems and culture to sustain and improve upon the changes made.

SORT – Sort through and sort out

How much of what is located in your work area is really needed? How much of it is there just because 'one day we may need it', or worse how much is there simply because no-one has removed it? The first step to implementing 5S is to sort the items that are needed from those that are not. One method of implementing SORT is to undertake a 'Red Tag Attack'. The purpose of this is to 'prune' the area of items that are not required so that it becomes both clearer and smarter. The 'Red Tag Attack' involves the team working in the area, along with a manager and where possible someone from another area who can bring a fresh pair of eyes. As the team move through the area they will see equipment, rubbish and stock. Any item that is not required, broken or simply unwanted is immediately 'red tagged'.

At the end of this process, the person responsible for each 'tagged' item is then consulted as to the reason why it should remain in the area. Acceptable reasons for items staying is that it is definitely used regularly or that removing it will introduce a patient safety risk. If an acceptable reason for keeping it is presented, the red tag should be removed. If there is doubt as to whether or not it will be required in that period, or if the next time it may be required is greater than a month away the red tag should remain on the item. At this time anything that is clearly rubbish should be disposed of.

Remaining 'red tagged' items should be removed from the area into a temporary holding area until they are proven that it is not required, normally up to around three months after first removing them. At this time the items can be disposed of or moved into longer-term storage.

The benefits of implementing SORT are that you will have less clutter and therefore less time spent searching for items and moving around obstacles. In addition, the work environment will look and feel more open. As mentioned above, many people stop at this point and therefore the association is made between 5S and housekeeping.

SET – Give items a logical home

Having removed all surplus items and rubbish from an area, the next step is to organise the area efficiently. Often this can be achieved by simply moving items closer together so that less time is spent walking between clinic rooms, receptions, wards and storage areas, etc. One way to help visualise what is really going on (and therefore what could be improved) is to use a 'spaghetti' or 'string' diagram to help you see the problem as shown below.

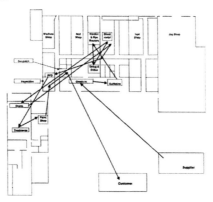

The figure previous shows a typical layout of a process after a SORT activity has been completed.

Drawn onto the layout is the flow of an individual between the different areas in the process. It is obvious that there is a significant amount of wasted time spent walking or carrying items between areas and also from searching for items.

By analysing the flow it is possible to relocate items so that they are located closer together to reduce walking distances and searching times. You may even identify further items that are not required and can be removed.

After redesigning the process to improve the flow and give things a logical home, it is common to define 'SET locations' for all needed items so that they don't stray. This can include the use of 'shadow boards', colour coding for easy recognition or floor/shelf/ rack markings to indicate what is supposed to be where.

Through just this simple exercise travel distances can be reduced by up to 90% and productivity increased by 10–30%, mostly by reducing searching times.

SHINE – Keep it clean

Having sorted out unneeded items and then improved what remains, the next stage is a thorough clean up and to put in place processes to keep it clean as well as ensuring that all items are returned to the SET locations at the end of every shift or day. This is sometimes achieved through a routine '5-Minute SHINE' at the end of each shift or day.

STANDARDISE – Make problems visible

STANDARDISE is about having defined processes that support the first 3S's so that mistakes cannot occur. This could include items already mentioned such as the daily 5-minute shine, shadow boards or the use of marked zones for storing items. Alternatively, it could include a set time every day or week to practise the first 3S's from top to bottom. By having simple, easy to follow processes and procedures it makes it harder for people to make mistakes and ensures the improvements remain embedded.

SUSTAIN – Stick to it

Although results can be achieved very quickly by the use of 5S, to continue to benefit from it there must be self-discipline. 5S requires managers to go back and re-visit work previously done for further improvements as well as ensuring that the STANDARDISE systems are maintained and monitored.

SUSTAIN is about the mental and physical disciplines required to maintain the other 4S items. Often people achieve the 'discipline' to maintain 5S through the use of routines, including self assessments, audits and checklists with the results visually displayed and regularly reviewed.

SUMMARY

The successful implementation of 5S requires everyone to understand why it is being used and what the expected results are, as the removal of familiar (although unneeded) items and the reorganisation of processes can be extremely unsettling if not properly communicated.

This may need to be coupled with training in the principles of 5S. Simply implementing SORT can have rapid results that demonstrate an organisation's commitment to change, whilst the application of the other elements can dramatically improve productivity and reduce both Waste and Lead Time.

The use of SORT and SIMPLIFY are excellent methods for involving people very early on in the change process. Often they find the experience to be exciting and fun and in this way it can be used to create a pool of people who are both positive and motivated about change and that is good for everyone!

CPSIA information can be obtained at www.ICGtesting.com
Printed in the USA
LVOW10s1607230914

405475LV00001B/23/P